THE
PASSION
TRANSLATION

THE PASSIONATE LIFE BIBLE STUDY SERIES

12-LESSON STUDY GUIDE

THE BOOK OF

PROVERBS

wisdom from above

BroadStreet
PUBLISHING

BroadStreet Publishing® Group, LLC
Savage, Minnesota, USA
BroadStreetPublishing.com

TPT: The Book of Proverbs: 12-Lesson Study Guide
Copyright © 2022 BroadStreet Publishing Group

978-1-4245-6437-8 (softcover)
978-1-4245-6438-5 (e-book)

Stock or custom editions of BroadStreet Publishing titles may be purchased in bulk for educational, business, ministry, fundraising, or sales promotional use. For information, please email info@broadstreetpublishing.com.

General editor: Brian Simmons
Managing editor: William D. Watkins
Writer: Jeremy Bouma

Design and typesetting by Garborg Design Works | garborgdesign.com

Printed in the China

22 23 24 25 26 5 4 3 2 1

Contents

From God's Heart to Yours

"God is love," says the apostle John, and "Everyone who loves is fathered by God and experiences an intimate knowledge of him" (1 John 4:7). The life of a Christ-follower is, at its core, a life of love—God's love of us, our love of him, and our love of others and ourselves because of God's love for us.

And this divine love is reliable, trustworthy, unconditional, other-centered, majestic, forgiving, redemptive, patient, kind, and more precious than anything else we can ever receive or give. It characterizes each person of the Trinity—Father, Son, and Holy Spirit—and so is as limitless as they are. They love one another with this eternal love, and they reach beyond themselves to us, created in their image with this love.

How do we know such incredible truths? Through the primary source of all else we know about the one God—his Word, the Bible. Of course, God reveals who he is through other sources as well, such as the natural world, miracles, our inner life, our relationships (especially with him), those who minister on his behalf, and those who proclaim him to us and others. But the fullest and most comprehensive revelation we have of God and from him is what he has given us in the thirty-nine books of the Hebrew Scriptures (the Old Testament) and the twenty-seven books of the Christian Scriptures (the New Testament). Together, these sixty-six books present a compelling and telling portrait of God and his dealings with us.

It is these Scriptures that *The Passionate Life Bible Study Series* is all about. Through these study guides, we—the editors and writers of this series—seek to provide you with a unique and welcoming opportunity to delve more deeply into God's precious Word, encountering there his loving heart for you and all the others he loves. God wants you to know him more deeply, to love him more devoutly, and to share his heart with others more frequently and freely. To accomplish this, we have based this study guide series on The Passion Translation of the Bible, which strives to "reintroduce the passion and fire of the Bible to the English reader. It doesn't merely convey the literal meaning of words. It expresses God's passion for people and his world by translating the original, life-changing message of God's Word for modern readers." It has been created to "kindle in you a burning desire to know the heart of God, while impacting the church for years to come."[1]

In each study guide, you will find an introduction to the Bible book it covers. There you will gain information about that Bible book's authorship, date of composition, first recipients, setting, purpose, central message, and key themes. Each lesson following the introduction will take a portion of that Bible book and walk you through it so you will learn its content better while experiencing and applying God's heart for your own life and encountering ways you can share his heart with others. Along the way, you will come across a number of features we have created that provide opportunities for more life application and growth in biblical understanding.

 ## Experience God's Heart

This feature focuses questions on personal application. It will help you live out God's Word and to bring the Bible into your world in fresh, exciting, and relevant ways.

 ## Share God's Heart

This feature will help you grow in your ability to share with other people what you learn and apply in a given lesson. It provides guidance on using the lesson to grow closer to others and to enrich your fellowship with others. It also points the way to enabling you to better listen to the stories of others so you can bridge the biblical story with their stories.

The Backstory

This feature provides ancient historical and cultural background that illuminates Bible passages and teachings. It deals with then-pertinent religious groups, communities, leaders, disputes, business trades, travel routes, customs, nations, political factions, ancient measurements and currency...in short, anything historical or cultural that will help you better understand what Scripture says and means.

 Word Wealth

This feature provides definitions for and other illuminating information about key terms, names, and concepts, and how different ancient languages have influenced the biblical text. It also provides insight into the different literary forms in the Bible, such as prophecy, poetry, narrative history, parables, and letters, and how knowing the form of a text can help you better interpret and apply it. Finally, this feature highlights the most significant passages in a Bible book. You may be encouraged to memorize these verses or keep them before you in some way so you can actively hide God's Word in your heart.

 Digging Deeper

This feature explains the theological significance of a text or the controversial issues that arise and mentions resources you can use to help you arrive at your own conclusions. Another way to dig deeper into the Word is by looking into the life of a biblical character or another person from church history, showing how that man or woman incarnated a biblical truth or passage. For instance, Jonathan Edwards was well known for his missions work among native American Indians and for his intellectual prowess in articulating the Christian faith, Florence Nightingale for the reforms she brought about in healthcare, Irenaeus for his fight against heresy, Billy Graham for his work in evangelism, Moses for the strength God gave him to lead the Hebrews and receive and communicate the law, and Deborah for her work as a judge in Israel. This feature introduces to you figures from the past who model what it looks like to experience God's heart and share his heart with others.

The Extra Mile

While The Passion Translation's notes are extensive, sometimes students of Scripture like to explore more on their own. In this feature, we provide you with opportunities to glean more information from a Bible dictionary, a Bible encyclopedia, a reliable Bible online tool, another ancient text, and the like. Here you will learn how you can go the extra mile on a Bible lesson. And not just in study either. Reflection, prayer, discussion, and applying a passage in new ways provide even more opportunities to go the extra mile. Here you will find questions to answer and applications to make that will require more time and energy from you—if and when you have them to give.

As you can see above, each of these features has a corresponding icon so you can quickly and easily identify them.

You will find other helps and guidance through the lessons of these study guides, including thoughtful questions, application suggestions, and spaces for you to record your own reflections, answers, and action steps. Of course, you can also write in your own journal, notebook, computer document, or other resource, but we have provided you with space for your convenience.

Also, each lesson will direct you toward the introductory material and numerous notes provided in The Passion Translation. There each Bible book contains a number of aids supplied to help you better grasp God's words and his incredible love, power, knowledge, plans, and so much more. We want you to get the most out of your Bible study, especially using it to draw you closer to the One who loves you most.

Finally, at the end of each lesson you'll find a section called "Talking It Out." This contains questions and exercises for application that you can share, answer, and apply with your spouse, a friend, a coworker, a Bible study group, or any other individuals or groups who would like to walk with you through this material. As Christians, we gather together to serve, study, worship, sing, evangelize, and a host of other activities. We grow together, not just on our own. This section will give you ample opportunities to engage others with some of the content of each lesson so you can work it out in community.

We offer all of this to support you in becoming an even more faithful and loving disciple of Jesus Christ. A disciple in the ancient world was a student of her teacher, a follower of his master. Students study, and followers follow. Jesus' disciples are to sit at his feet and listen and learn and then do what he tells them and shows them to do. We have created *The Passionate Life Bible Study Series* to help you do what a disciple of Jesus is called to do.

So go.

Read God's words.

Hear what he has to say in them and through them.

Meditate on them.

Hide them in your heart.

Display their truths in your life.

Share their truths with others.

Let them ignite Jesus' passion and light in all you say and do.

Use them to help you fulfill what Jesus called his disciples to do: "Now wherever you go, make disciples of all nations, baptizing them in the name of the Father, the Son, and the Holy Spirit. And teach them to faithfully follow all that I have commanded you. And never forget that I am with you every day, even to the completion of this age" (Matthew 28:19–20).

And through all of this, let Jesus' love nourish your heart and allow that love to overflow into your relationships with others (John 15:9–13). For it was for love that Jesus came, served, died, rose from the dead, and ascended into heaven. This love he gives us. And this love he wants us to pass along to others.

Why I Love the Book of Proverbs

As a new believer, I was told that if I wanted wisdom and to succeed in life, I needed to read and study the book of Proverbs. That was some of the best advice I've ever received. Now fifty years later, I still find pleasure in reading these poetic verses. They are powerful and potent. Something is released inside of me when I read this book.

I love Proverbs, for it speaks to me right where I am. It isn't a book filled with lofty prose or lengthy doctrinal lectures. It is a voice that speaks gut-level to everyone who wants to follow the ways of God. It can puncture our pride and point us to the paths of righteousness. Proverbs has such powerful words that it can correct me in my error and stop me in my tracks. A daily dose of Proverbs has been known to cure the heart of presumption and foolishness. Solomon doesn't mince words with these thirty-one chapters of wisdom.

I love Proverbs because of the vivid contrasts it presents. Like virtue and vice, wisdom and folly, righteousness and wickedness, truth and deceit, humility and pride, joy and sorrow, generosity and greed, love and hate, justice and injustice, order and disorder, and purity and lust. Just about every problem known to man has a solution in the book of Proverbs. It is like a flaming arrow shot into our hearts meant to ignite us with love and devotion for God.

Have you noticed that Proverbs speaks to you in every season of life? We find truth about raising children, loving wisdom, listening to the wise, earning a living, relationships, old age, and living virtuously. From the cradle to the grave, Proverbs has wisdom to guide us.

And finally, I love Proverbs because it speaks truth to power. Those who are in leadership with a measure of authority over others can learn how to lead with a clean heart. Yes, it will rebuke us when we are wrong, but it will also console us as we walk humbly with God, leaning on the sacred wisdom it presents.

I hope you'll enjoy your journey through this road map for life. I know it will bring you closer to God. May the wisdom from above that is pure, peaceable, and powerful guide your steps each day until we gather around heaven's glorious throne!

Brian Simmons
General Editor

LESSON 1

Proverbs

A Wisdom Primer

You are about to encounter a book offering ancient Hebrew wisdom straight from the heart of God, the book of Proverbs. It offers powerful insight from the very throne room of God that will guide your steps and direct your life.

Wisdom guides us along life's way by offering signposts of God's abundant life for a myriad of challenges that can be confusing to navigate. Need help overcoming anger, pride, or greed—or perhaps you'd like to be a more controlled, generous, joy-filled person? There's counsel from Proverbs for all the above. Are you a parent desperate for advice on training your child or a friend seeking guidance to foster peaceful relationships? Turn to Proverbs. From questions about truth and deceit, wealth and poverty, living an ordered and disordered life, and finding joy instead of despair, God generously pours out his wisdom through this book for all who seek it.

Whether religious or not, anyone seeking practical advice for human flourishing and a fulfilling life will find what they are longing for in this book. This isn't to say there is no theological value in Proverbs. Because as Solomon insists straight away: "We cross the threshold of true knowledge when we live in obedient devotion to God" (Proverbs 1:7). Although it may appear that many of the words of wisdom have no theological value on their own, every word of the book signals the way to God's abundant life envisioned for humanity. This wisdom can be valued for wisdom's sake, not merely for the sake of religious commitment, and yet Proverbs makes it clear that God is wisdom's source. You will find insight into the heart of God and his way of life in these words.

The book of Proverbs offers "a new way of writing," explained John Wesley, the great English Methodist evangelist, "wherein Divine wisdom is taught us in Proverbs...And these Proverbs of Solomon are not merely a collection of the wise sayings which had been formerly delivered, but were the dictates of the Spirit of God in Solomon: so that it is God by Solomon that here speaks to us." In other words: these words of Solomon are God's words! And the scope of every word is "to direct us so to order our conversation, that we may see the salvation of God."[2]

What you learn from this book will change your life and launch you into your destiny. Listening to its words means listening to the very voice of God himself. His words never return unfulfilled whether in your life or in the lives of those you know, for "[Yahweh's] word performs my purpose and fulfills the mission I sent it out to accomplish" (Isaiah 55:11).

Authorship

One could make the case that Proverbs is the greatest book of wisdom ever written, penned mostly by the wisest man who ever lived. God gave Solomon this wisdom to pass along to us, God's servants, who continue the ministry of Jesus, the embodiment of wisdom, until he returns in full glory. While Solomon penned most of these words of wisdom, it is believed others had a hand too, including advisers to King Hezekiah and the unknown men Agur and Lemuel—which could be pseudonyms for Solomon. Regardless, the one who edited the final version of Proverbs brought together the wisest teachings from the wisest person ever to have lived, writing a book that contains some of the deepest revelation-insights into God's way of wisdom in the Bible. When Solomon pens a proverb, there is more to it than meets the eye.

- *Do you have someone in your life whom you consider wise? Who is it? And what have you received from him or her that you find wise?*

Date of Composition

The book of Proverbs was composed during the tenth to fifth centuries BC. It was meant as a sort of manual for practically living out the moral law of Israel, directing the hearts of its readers back to Yahweh in worship while offering insights into living a useful and effective life.

The genre of this book is known as Wisdom Literature, something that was common during the time period of ancient Israel, ranging from the Egyptians to the Sumerians of Mesopotamia as well as the Assyrians. Many of the specific topics covered in this book share parallels with these words of wisdom from different ancient peoples. However, what we find in this biblical book is quite different, the special ingredient that is the key to opening up God's wisdom: a personal relationship through faith with the very personal God of the Israelites, Yahweh, is the foundation of living the kind of life reflected in these wise words.

God opened his loving heart of wisdom to Solomon and other authors of Proverbs in order to empower you to experience his heart to its fullest in the most personal of ways: living the abundant life he intended through wisdom, driven by faith in and a holy awe of Yahweh.

- *What might it tell you about the nature of wisdom that it appears so universally, spanning the known world during the time Proverbs was composed?*

- *What is the special "ingredient" that opens up the wisdom of God found in the biblical book of Proverbs? How does it differ from the wisdom of the world?*

- *Why might this difference be so crucial to reigning in life and succeeding in our divine destiny?*

Recipients of Proverbs

These nuggets of the choicest of wisdom were written from God's heart to yours. Throughout the book we find words like "Listen, my sons. Listen, my daughters." The book of Proverbs is written to us as sons and daughters of the living God with the same loving care that an earthly father might provide when sharing words of wisdom with his children. The teaching we receive is not from a distant god who tells us we'd better live right or else. These are personal words of love and tenderness from our wise heavenly Father, the Father of all eternity, who speaks right into our hearts with radiant words of healing, power, and dominion. You are invited to receive deeply these words of our kind Father as though he were speaking directly to you—because he is!

- *As a recipient of these wise words from above, consider what sort of godly counsel you currently desire for your life. Make a list of topics for which you hope to glean insights over the course of this study.*

Setting and Purpose

The book of Proverbs was gifted from God's heart to each of ours to help all people gain wisdom and knowledge, to avoid folly, and discover the abundant life of God. It serves as a collection of ancient Hebrew wisdom, guiding us out of foolishness and into prudent living and exhorting us to embrace the fear of the Lord.

As the opening verse explains: Proverbs contains "words to live by, and words of wisdom given to empower you to reign in life."

- *Read Proverbs 1:1–7, arguably the purpose statement from the author himself. What do you learn there about the purpose of Proverbs? You may find more than one purpose for these wise sayings.*

These proverbs can be interpreted in their most literal and practical sense, following their guidance for everyday living. However, we cannot tap into the wisdom contained in them through a casual, surface reading. The Spirit has breathed upon every verse illuminations that offer a deeper meaning of practical insight to guide our steps into the lives God meant for us to live. Since there is often both a literal and a practical sense along with a deeper meaning of insight embedded in these proverbs, it is important to let this principle guide your approach to this book.

- *For example, a surface reading of Proverbs 6:6–7 would tell us that ants are self-sufficient and self-starters. How might a deeper reading encourage your walk?*

- *Similarly, consider 5:15–18. What does a deeper reading have to say about issues of purity and pleasure?*

What Is a Proverb?

The nature of Hebrew poetry is quite different from that of English poetry. There is a pleasure found in Hebrew poetry that transcends rhyme and meter. The Hebrew verses come in a poetic package, a form of meaning that imparts an understanding that is deeper than mere logic. True revelation unfolds an encounter, an experience of knowing God often as he is revealed through the mysterious vocabulary of riddle, proverb, and parable.

🅝 WORD WEALTH

The Hebrew word for "proverb," *mashal*, has two meanings. The first is "parable, byword, metaphor, a pithy saying that expresses wisdom." But the second meaning is overlooked by many. The homonym *mashal* can also mean "to rule, to take dominion" or "to reign with power."[3]

- *In your own words, how would you explain the meaning of a proverb, according to the original Hebrew?*

- *What makes it different from the way God gave us revelation-insight in the Pentateuch, the Gospels, or Paul's letters?*

- *Why do you suppose God gave us these nuggets of truth in this sort of poetic manner in Proverbs?*

DIGGING DEEPER

The ancients had a keener sense of what a proverb was. Consider how the early church writer Didymus the Blind explained the meaning of "proverb":

> A proverb is a saying such as, "War is pleasant to the inexperienced," or "A drop constantly falling hollows a stone." The name proverb derived from the fact that once roads were marked off with no signs. Now there are signs, which are called *miliaria* (milestones) by the Romans, while they were just called signs before. Ancient

people set them in certain places and then inscribed them with certain information and questions. So they fulfilled two purposes. On the one hand, they indicated to the traveler the length of the journey. On the other, when one read the inscription and kept busy comprehending it, one was relieved of weariness. Therefore a road is called in Greek *oimos*, from which is derived the word *paroimia*, which means "proverb."[4]

- *How does this nugget of insight from the early church writer expand and enhance your understanding of the essence of a proverb?*

- *Connect the purpose a proverb has in your life to the two purposes a road sign had in ancient days. How do these function in your own life?*

Key Themes from Proverbs

The book of Proverbs offers insight from above, straight from the fountain of God's well of wisdom, to anyone who is interested. This book weaves together several themes that are all rooted in the fear of the Lord, which we will explore more deeply in the next lesson. One of the ways to explore the book is through contrasts, similar to how we might understand virtues and vices.

Although there are several themes (some Christian writers even catalogued over one hundred), we will examine eleven virtue–vice contrasts: wisdom and folly, righteousness and wickedness, truth and deceit, humility and pride, joy and sorrow, generosity and greed, love and hate, justice and injustice, order and disorder, and purity and pleasure.

- *Which of these key themes of Proverbs are you most interested in learning about?*

- *Which do you suppose will be the most challenging for you personally?*

 DIGGING DEEPER

Throughout Proverbs, we find wisdom being personified with a unique metaphor: Lady Wisdom, who dispenses revelation-knowledge and living-understanding to those willing to listen. Lady Wisdom is a figure of speech for God and his divine wisdom, who invites us to receive the best way to live, the excellent and noble way of life.

Read through the sampling of passages from Proverbs below, which personify wisdom and offer insight into its role in our lives. Then list some key observations about the nature of Lady Wisdom:

6:22

7:4

8:1–3

9:1–6

Jesus and Proverbs

As with the rest of the Old Testament, we are called to read the book of Proverbs in light of Jesus and his ministry. Consider that throughout the Gospels, Jesus is associated with wisdom. For instance, in Matthew 11:18–19 Jesus claims his actions represent Lady Wisdom herself. Elsewhere, in Mark 1:22, "The people were awestruck by his teaching, because he taught in a way that demonstrated God's authority, which was quite unlike the religious scholars." Still further in Mark 6:2, we see the people said of Jesus, "What incredible wisdom has been given to him! Where did he receive such profound insights?" This identification with wisdom is a powerful way of saying that Jesus is the full, entire embodiment of Lady Wisdom.

You can find shades of this connection between Jesus and Lady Wisdom in Colossians 1:15–17 and Proverbs 8:24–31. Likewise, the preface to John's Gospel in 1:1–3 resonates with this same chapter when Jesus is associated with the Word, another personification of wisdom.

- *Read Proverbs 8, John 1:1–3, and Colossians 1:15–17. What parallels do you notice between these three passages, particularly the firstborn nature of both Jesus and Lady Wisdom?*

The Core Message

If there was ever a time to dive deep into the pool of God's overflowing wisdom, now is the time to suit up and strap on the goggles. More than ever, we need words to live by that "empower [us] to reign in life" (Proverbs 1:1) and "unlock the treasures of true knowledge" (v. 2). Thankfully, there is a way into this life and these treasures. God calls out to us and the world through these words that have "greater worth than gold and treasure" (8:19). Words of wisdom that transcend cultures and shift not with time.

 EXPERIENCE GOD'S HEART

- *How have you experienced the heart of God already through the book of Proverbs, perhaps either through his correction from past misdeeds or through his guidance as you've lived your life?*

- *How might God want to open up his heart of love to you through the wisdom contained in the book of Proverbs, offering continued correction and guidance for where you are in your journey?*

♥ SHARE GOD'S HEART

- *Part of what it means to be a Christian is to be available and faithful vessels through which God speaks to others about himself—just as Solomon was in writing down God's revelation-insight into the kind of life Yahweh wants for us. In what ways can you similarly share with the world around you what God has spoken to you personally about this way of wisdom? Take time to memorize some of the Proverbs in the coming weeks to pass along to unbelievers as the situation warrants.*

- *"I'm calling to you, sons of Adam," Proverbs 8:4–5 says, "yes, and to you daughters as well. Listen to me and you will be prudent and wise. For even the foolish and feeble can receive an understanding heart that will change their inner being." Who are the sons and daughters of Adam in your life who need to listen to Lady Wisdom? Are you among them? Pray now and over the coming lessons for opportunities to recognize and share the heart of God found in these words.*

Talking It Out

Since Christians grow in community, not just in solitude, here are some questions you may want to discuss with another person or in a group. Each "Talking It Out" section is designed with this purpose in mind.

1. Read through the entire book of Proverbs in one sitting. As you approach the study of this matchless book, what are your biggest questions based on what you read? What most confuses you? Pray for guidance in the coming weeks that God would impart his knowledge from his Word to your heart.

2. Do you have a single or handful of favorite nuggets of wisdom from the book of Proverbs that you have memorized or keep written down close at hand? If so, share one or two, and explain why they are so meaningful to you.

3. What part has wisdom in general played in your life? Do you feel you are a wise person and make wise decisions, or is there room for improvement?

LESSON 2

Wisdom's Foundation

The Fear of the Lord

In 1961, Vincent Lombardi walked into the Green Bay Packer's locker room at the start of training camp ready to get his players into shape for the coming season. But first, he had a little message to get their heads in the game.

Taking up a pigskin in his right hand, he held out the ball and uttered five words that would become iconic not only in the world of sports but also in the world of life: "Gentlemen, this is a football."

Odd way to launch a training season, no doubt, given he was standing before three dozen professional athletes who nearly won the Super Bowl game the year before. And yet there Lombardi was, starting with the most basic element of the game. The football.

The way a biographer explained it: "He took nothing for granted. He began a tradition of starting from scratch, assuming that the players were blank slates who carried over no knowledge from the year before...He began with the most elemental statement of all."[5] The fundamentals were important to understanding the game of football, and that's where Lombardi began. Get the foundation right, you get the game right. That's what Lombardi understood and what he wanted his players to understand.

The author of Proverbs begins the same way, drawing our attention to the most foundational element undergirding every element of this brilliant tome of wisdom: the fear of the Lord.

From the beginning, Proverbs makes it clear that we gain the essence of wisdom and "cross the threshold of true knowledge" only when we *fear the Lord*—or, as The Passion Translation reads, when we live "in obedient devotion to God" (1:7).

Living in a way such that our entire being worships and adores God is a constant theme throughout Proverbs. It is fundamental for gaining and keeping wisdom. The fear of the Lord is the "football" of life.

Getting that foundation right is crucial to getting the game of life right.

Fear of the Lord Is Not Fearing the Lord

Throughout the book of Proverbs, the *fear of the Lord* is a major theme that appears almost in every chapter in some way. But we need to be clear about what the book has in mind: *fear* is not the same as *fearing*. We're not talking about dread or anxiety. Instead, you could describe it as *reverential awe*. This awe is what grounds our pursuit of knowledge and our understanding of wisdom. The orientation of our life around the Lord, what motivates and drives us, is what unlocks knowledge, understanding, and wisdom of his good, blessed life.

🔴 WORD WEALTH

The original Hebrew word for "fear" is *yir'ah*. As a note in The Passion Translation explains:

> Many translations render this "the fear of the Lord." [However,] this means much more than the English concept of fear. It also implies submission, awe, worship, and reverence. The Hebrew word used here is found fourteen times in Proverbs. The number fourteen represents spiritual

perfection...It is also the number for Passover. You will pass from darkness to wisdom's light by the "fear" of the Lord.[6]

• *There are plenty of examples in the Bible where God shows up and someone has a radical encounter with him and his heart. We find such an encounter in Genesis 28:10–22. Read this passage and retell in your own words what happened. What did Jacob do afterward, and how do you suppose he felt about his encounter with God, even though it was just in a dream and not face-to-face. What does this event convey to you about the fear of the Lord?*

THE BACKSTORY

Fear of the Lord is a deeply theological concept that has roots in the original religious setting of the Israelites during the reign of Solomon and later after the exile. John Walton and Andrew Hill offer insightful background:

> The "fear of the Lord" is the way Israelites expressed what was at the center of their worldview. In the polytheistic setting of the ancient world, it was not unusual for the people to believe in the existence of many gods. Even some Israelites would have believed that other gods existed. So

it would not be enough for the Israelites to center their worldview on the belief in Yahweh. Fear of Yahweh meant that they worshiped him and that they embraced the unique nature of Yahweh as it had been revealed to them. That is, the "fear of the Lord" assumed the adoption of the picture of Yahweh as distinct from the ways that their neighbors imagined their gods. Consequently, an Israelite saying that he "feared Yahweh" would be making a worldview statement at the same level of someone today identifying herself as a theist, deist, agnostic, or atheist.[7]

There were considerable worldview ramifications of an Israelite taking a "fear of the Lord" mindset in the ancient Near East. One would be that the Hebrews feared God because they knew he was real and that the other gods people believed in were not. Another ramification would be that fearing the Lord meant that they knew Yahweh was greater, more fearsome than any other power around.

- *Consider your own world and the ramifications of posturing your life in awe-filled worship and fear of the Lord. What kind of worldview statement would you be making, and what impact might that make in your life, especially with those who are closest to you?*

# DIGGING DEEPER

Many of the earliest Christian thinkers understood that "fear of the Lord" implied a life of piety and virtue; a life lived in the fear of the Lord is oriented toward righteous living. Consider the fourth-century archbishop of Constantinople John Chrysostom's explanation of the verse:

> Piety toward God is a beginning [of
> discernment]. It acts as a fountain and
> source for discerning the divine, according
> to our inner being, so that we may see
> the true light, hear the secret oracles, be
> nourished with the bread of life, obtain the
> fragrance of Christ and learn the doctrine
> of this life. When we have piety, our senses
> too are allied with us, when neither our
> eyes see nor our mouth speaks evil.[8]

It doesn't stop there, for "fear of the Lord" is concerned with moving away from wickedness and evil. Ambrose, Bishop of Milan and a fourth-century theologian, exhorted, "He who fears the Lord departs from error and directs his ways to the path of virtue. Except a man fear the Lord, he is unable to renounce sin."[9] There is also a religious element to this fear, where belief in and knowledge of God is necessary. Theodore of Cyrus, a fifth-century theologian, argued, "To the atheist is the name fool most accurately applied in truth and nature: if the fear of God is the beginning of wisdom, lack of fear and denial of him would be the opposite of wisdom."[10]

- *In light of these observations from our ancient Christian ancestors, why does the fear of the Lord matter to our lives? What is its significance to how we should live?*

Know God, Fear God

A genuine posture of awe-filled worship and fear of God is at least partly based on one's genuine knowledge of God. Who stands in awe and wonder before a vague impression of what God might be like? One fears what one has good reason to fear, whether that reason is rational or not. But Scripture fosters a rational fear of God because of what it teaches about who and what God is.

He is all-powerful, before whom our power seems puny. He is all-knowing, before whom our knowledge seems paltry. He is everywhere present, so we can't run from him, hide from him, or deceive him. The more we understand God, his attributes and character, his power and wonders, the more we stand in fearful awe of him. We are nothing before him—except for his love. We have full access to come before him and know we are accepted and won't be crushed.

Which makes possessing real, genuine knowledge of the true awesomeness of God vital for awe-filled worship—leading to an understanding of the Lord's wise ways and his wise life. Such knowledge flows not only from reading and studying his Word but also from walking with him through life experiences that build trust and beckon worship. After all, as the hymn of old declares, "How I've proved him o'er and o'er!"[11]

- *How much do you truly know God, understanding his power and wonders, his love and holiness? We all have room to grow, but are you a so-called baby Christian, or have you known God for years?*

- *Where do you feel you lack in that understanding, and where do you want to grow? What is your plan for growing in that knowledge?*

Seek and Search

One of the ways the author of Proverbs frames fear of the Lord is the nature of our pursuit of it. Proverbs seems to be as concerned, or more, with this pursuit as it is with how we pursue knowledge itself. Consider Proverbs 2:4–5: "For if you keep seeking [wisdom] like a man would seek for sterling silver, searching in hidden places for cherished treasure, then you will discover the fear of the Lord and find the true knowledge of God."

EXPERIENCE GOD'S HEART

- *The author uses two imperatives here when it comes to the fear of the Lord: seek and search. Consider your own pursuit of the heart of God with humility and awe. Do you seek after it as you would silver and search for it as cherished treasure? Are you as consumed with awe in worship of Yahweh as you are in attaining knowledge and wisdom?*

The Bitter Fruit of No Fear

"Because you have turned up your nose at me and closed your eyes to the facts and refused to worship me in awe—because you scoffed at my wise counsel and laughed at my correction—now you will eat the bitter fruit of your own ways" (1:29–31). This passage articulates what happens when one not only scoffs at wisdom but when one's heart also refuses "to worship me in awe," or have proper "fear of the Lord." Again, "the Hebrew word used here can be translated 'fear,' 'dread,' 'awe,' or 'worship.' Nearly every translation uses the word *fear* or *reverence* while ignoring the other aspects of the Aramaic word *dekhlatha*."[12]

- *This verse promises that people who spurn such fear "will eat the bitter fruit of your own ways." What do you suppose the author means by this? Why might lacking fear and awe of Yahweh result in us reaping bitter fruit?*

Wisdom's Calling

"Wisdom pours into you when you begin to hate every form of evil in your life, for that's what worship and fearing God is all about. Then you will discover that your pompous pride and perverse speech are the very ways of wickedness that I hate!" (8:13). In this passage, the author further unveils what worshiping and fearing God is all about.

- *What does this passage teach?*

- *What would this look like in your daily life?*

- *Are there any changes you need to make? If so, what are they?*

Wisdom's Security

"Confidence and strength flood the hearts of the lovers of God who live in awe of him, and their devotion provides their children with a place of shelter and security" (14:26). Consider the early church father Augustine's commentary on this verse:

> *"The fear of the Lord is the hope of courage."* When you fear the punishment that is threatened, you learn to love the reward that is promised; and thus through fear of punishment you keep on leading a good life, and by leading a good life you acquire a good conscience, so that finally through a good conscience you don't fear any punishment. Therefore, learn how to fear, if you don't want to be afraid.[13]

- *What insights can you glean from Augustine's explanation of this verse, and how can you specifically apply them to your own life?*

𝐧 WORD WEALTH

The proverbs teach that there is a security that comes from fearing the Lord, a confidence and strength from living in awe of him. The word that is used here for confidence, strength, security is *mivtach*. "The image is of a 'secure fortress' for the God-fearer and his children. The 'fear' finds expression in obedience to the law, with all of its rewards and punishments, and this obedience ensures safety."[14]

- *Why do you suppose the writer connects fear of the Lord to strength and security in this way?*

- *Why is such a life filled with the awe of God like a secure fortress? What security does it offer those whose position before God is one of awe?*

Wisdom's Promise

A wonderful, rich hymn offers an anthem for every Christian:

> Standing, standing
> Standing on the promises of God my Savior
> Standing, standing
> I'm standing on the promises of God.[15]

The Bible is filled with a constant stream of promises from the Lord to his children. By one estimate, you can count over two thousand of them! Proverbs 19:23 is one of those verses we can stand on: "When you live a life of abandoned love, surrendered before the awe of God, here's what you'll experience: Abundant life. Continual protection. And complete satisfaction!" Here again, the writer is turning our attention to wisdom's foundation: awe-filled worship and fear of the Lord.

- *Explain what sort of promise this verse offers. In other words, what are we to do to receive these promises?*

- *Now reflect on the three promised rewards. What does each one mean?*

- *Are you experiencing any of these three promises? If so, to what degree? If not, do you have any ideas why that is?*

- *Do you know another believer who seems to have these promises even partially fulfilled in his or her life? If so, how are the promises manifesting themselves?*

- *Take some time before God to ask him to help you live a
  "life of abandoned love" with him. He wants this in your
  life, so this is a prayer he will certainly say yes to.*

🌙 SHARE GOD'S HEART

Sometimes others need the promises of God more than we do,
especially if they are living far from him—far from living a life in
fear of the Lord. Perhaps Proverbs 19:23 is one such verse, one
that can orient people whose lives are far from abundance and
satisfaction to make a course correction toward living a life abandoned and surrendered to God in complete awe.

- *Whom do you know in your life who needs this promise?
  How might it look to share with them the truth of it, opening
  their eyes to their need to live in the fear of the Lord?*

A Life of Humble Surrender

In 22:4, the author writes, "Laying your life down in tender surrender before the Lord will bring life, prosperity, and honor as your reward." Another way of saying this is, "The reward for humility and fear of Yahweh is riches and glory and life." It follows a word of wisdom cautioning the senseless fool who rushes blindly forward, suffering the consequences from his haste. The remedy is instead *humility*, "a religious term denoting the renunciation of human sufficiency, of the sort associated with the fear of the Lord."[16] In other words, the remedy for the way of the senseless fool is "Laying your life down in tender surrender before the Lord" in humility and in awe of God.

- *Why might humility and the fear of the Lord, laying down your life and surrendering before the Lord be inextricably linked?*

- *What are the rewards for such a lifestyle choice, and why do you suppose they naturally flow from a life surrendered in humility before the Lord with awe and fear?*

Wise Basics

Sometimes we need to get back to the basics of life; some-times we need a reminder of what a football is. The same holds true for our walk with the Lord, especially when we desire his wisdom and long to live the abundant, blessed life he has in store for us. Remember: the journey toward that life begins with living in awe of the One whose heart is open to yours. In the coming lessons, we will constantly bring the topics of exploration back to this foundation, this Christian-life basic. For without awe-filled worship, we have no hope for discovering and experiencing Yahweh's wisdom from above.

Talking It Out

1. The beginning of godly wisdom is the fear of the Lord. What is the starting place for wisdom outside of the Lord's teachings found in the Bible? Why does where your wisdom begin make a difference in where your wisdom ends up?

2. An example of a worldly proverb might be the soda slogan, "Obey your thirst." Brainstorm some others and examine the assumptions behind the proverb and where you see such "wisdom" ending.

3. Bottom line is that wisdom begins with a relationship with the Lord, where our heart is intimately and passionately connected to his own. Where are you in your own relationship with God? Where is there room to grow?

4. At the beginning, we made clear that "fear of the Lord" is not dread and anxiety about God but instead carries with it the implication of *submission*, *awe*, *worship*, and *reverence*. The Bible is filled with instances where someone had a radical encounter with God and his heart, like Jacob, and they were filled with awe and reverential wonder. Moses is another example with the burning bush, as is Paul on the road to Damascus. What about you? When did God show up in your life and leave you in awe-filled worship and wonder?

LESSON 3

Wisdom vs. Folly

There is a website associated with a popular book series based on the ancient wisdom tradition of Stoicism. DailyStoic.com features "ancient wisdom for everyday life." It describes this ancient wisdom as "a tool in the pursuit of self-mastery, perseverance, and wisdom: something one uses to live a great life, rather than some esoteric field of academic inquiry."[17]

Focusing on logic and ethics, "Stoicism took aim at the unpredictable nature of everyday life and offered a set of practical tools meant for daily use,"[18] providing answers to such questions as: What is the good life? How can I control my anger? What should I do with my wealth? How should I treat my neighbor? What does a well-ordered life look like, and how can I experience it?

Sound familiar?

Yet where do Stoics find the answers to these burning questions, the ones we all ask from time to time? Primarily in the musings of three prominent Romans: Marcus Aurelius, Seneca, and Epictetus, who were respectively an emperor, a political adviser, and a slave-turned-teacher. Although the most essential values of Stoicism are noteworthy—courage, temperance, justice, wisdom—they are rooted not in any transcendent revelation-truth but in the fallible minds of fallen men.

Biblical wisdom, however, is rooted in something far different. The Serenity Prayer, as it has been called and which is used by various iterations by Alcoholics Anonymous and similar recovery groups, offers an important reminder in which to ground our study of this most important topic:

> God, grant me the serenity
> to accept the things I cannot change,
> the courage to change the things I can,
> and the wisdom to know the difference.

Attributed to Reinhold Niebuhr, you'll notice this prayer is directed to God asking for help: *Grant me!* Niebuhr was an American Reformed theologian who knew the wisdom we needed for our everyday life comes not from the musings of dead ancient Romans. Instead, it flows from the generous heart of the Ancient of Days! And as we saw in the last lesson, we tap into this wisdom with a proper life orientation of awe-filled worship and fear of the Lord.

We're all looking for wisdom. None of us gets up in the morning and wants to live a foolish life. The trick is learning where to look in order to find true wisdom. James 1:5 reminds us: "If anyone longs to be wise, ask God for wisdom and he will give it!"

The Fear of the Lord
Is the Beginning of Wisdom

"We cross the threshold of true knowledge when we live in obedient devotion to God" (Proverbs 1:7). In other words, wise living starts with a proper mindset of awe-filled worship and fear of the Lord. This is true for wise living in all its forms. It's important at the start, then, to consider why our heart's orientation matters to this lesson on wisdom and folly.

- *What do wisdom and foolishness mean? Feel free to use a Bible dictionary or a website like www.biblestudytools. com but also give an initial definition from what you already understand.*

- *Now how do you suppose a proper posture before God, living in obedient devotion to him with healthy fear, leads to the wise life? Why does awe-filled worship orient our heart around the Lord's wisdom?*

- *Consider the opposite, when we refuse to worship Yahweh in awe and spurn reverential fear. How does this choice lead to a life of foolishness in a variety of ways? Why is refusing to fear God and worship him in awe the path of fools?*

Lady Wisdom and Living-Understanding

In the last lesson, we saw that *fear of the Lord* is the most foundational element of the book of Proverbs. We also pointed out a second important element: the theologically rich metaphor of Lady Wisdom. Throughout Proverbs, wisdom is personified by this figure of speech. Her divine wisdom invites us to receive the best way to live, the excellent and noble way of life. This figure represents Yahweh's wisdom as well as Yahweh himself, which makes wisdom in this book and the pursuit of it a deeply theological exercise.[19] God promises that revelation-knowledge will flow to the one who hungers for the gift of understanding (14:6), from his very heart to yours.

- *The book personifies wisdom in three specific sections:*
  1:20–33, 8:1–36, and 9:1–6. Read through each of the
  passages, noting how the author uses the personification
  of wisdom, Lady Wisdom, to reveal what God wants us to
  know. What does Lady Wisdom want to say to us? How
  should we respond?

Wisdom's Warning

In 1:20–33, we encounter the first call from Lady Wisdom out into the world, "a lovely woman inviting hungry people to a great feast."[20] Matthew Henry identifies the personification of wisdom with Christ himself, and he lists three kinds of people whom Christ calls out:

> 1.) Simple ones. Sinners are fond of their simple notions of good and evil, their simple prejudices against the ways of God, and flatter themselves in their wickedness. 2.) Scorners. Proud, jovial people, that make a jest of every thing. Scoffers at religion, that run down every thing sacred and serious. 3.) Fools. Those are the worst of fools that hate to be taught, and have a rooted dislike to serious godliness. The precept is plain: Turn you at my reproof. We do not make a right use of reproofs, if we do not turn from evil to that which is good.[21]

- *Do you find yourself in any of these three kinds of people, or do you know of anyone who fits any of these categories? Explain. What do you think Lady Wisdom wants to say to them or even to you?*

The Value of Wisdom

Proverbs 2:6–11 is a rich passage extolling the value of wisdom. It is announced by the opening verse: "Wisdom is a gift from a generous God, and every word he speaks is full of revelation and becomes a fountain of understanding within you."

• *Do you value wisdom? To what degree do you value it, and how is such value evident in your life?*

• *In what way is wisdom a gift, and how is it a generous one from a generous God? Give examples for each.*

Wisdom's Guidance

Proverbs 3:5–6 offers one of the most familiar sets of verses in the book, perhaps in the whole Bible. It is also some of the most profound wisdom for navigating life: "Trust in the Lord completely, and do not rely on your own opinions. With all your heart rely on him to guide you, and he will lead you in every decision you make. Become intimate with him in whatever you do, and he will lead you wherever you go."

Commentator Paul Koptak brings some remarkable vision to bear on this passage: "Trust is the antidote to autonomy, worry, and a preoccupation with holding and taking. Put another way, this chapter sets out trust as a way to learn how to love God, how to love the things of this world, and how to love other persons, keeping each in its proper place."[22]

- *How does this comment bring greater depth of insight into your understanding of this passage—and your experience of God's heart through trusting in him completely?*

- *Why is trust vital when it comes to living a wise life? Do you trust that God's way is the wisest—especially in contrast to the foolishness of the world? Or are you trusting in a different source for wisdom? Explain.*

Alongside this positive admonition to trust in Yahweh completely with the promise of guidance, there is a negative one: "Don't think for a moment that you know it all, for wisdom comes when you adore him with undivided devotion and avoid everything that's wrong" (3:7).

- *When it comes to trusting the Lord's wisdom, where do you fall on a scale of 1 to 10—where leaning into Yahweh with a fully trusting heart is a 10 and seeking wisdom from within is a 1? In what areas do you trust him the most to guide how you live? How about the least?*

- *Spend some time assessing where you fall on this scale, committing to trust in the Lord more fully, not relying on your own opinions.*

A Father's Instructions on Wisdom's Way

Read Proverbs 4:1–19. Although the plural "sons" in the opening verse suggests student disciples are in view, with the "father" as teacher, "the fact that the teacher-pupil relationship was modeled on the parent-child relationship suggests that a father-children relationship is indicated," especially since "mother" is used in verse 3.[23] A father is reaching out again to dispense wisdom to his children, urging them to embrace wisdom's way and all of its benefits.

This figure of a roadway is used to compare "walking or running on a safe road, a course that will be free of obstacles, so that progress will lead to abundant life" in contrast to a different path, a "lifestyle with a path that can be traveled—only now the lifestyle is evil, masquerading as what is true and right."[24]

- *Make a chart of these two divergent paths, explaining the benefits of wisdom's way contrasted with the folly of the way of the wicked.*

 EXPERIENCE GOD'S HEART

In the previous chapter, Yahweh himself is pictured in 3:11–12 as a loving father who speaks to us with wise words and whose "discipline comes only from his passionate love and pleasure for you."

With that in mind, read Proverbs 4:1–19 again. This time, read it as though your heavenly Father himself were speaking to you as his son or daughter. For as 1 John 3:1 reminds us, "Look with wonder at the depth of the Father's marvelous love that he has lavished on us! He has called us and made us his very own beloved children."

• *What from this passage do you think your Father wants to impart to you concerning wisdom and understanding in order to experience his heart fully?*

♥ SHARE GOD'S HEART

The lessons of wisdom found in Proverbs and all of life are meant to be passed along from parents to their children. If you are a parent, you know how difficult it can be to raise boys and girls into good and godly men and women. Yet what parents don't want this for their own child? What parents don't want to bestow upon their children the wisdom they themselves have discovered through life's ups and downs?

• *Like the father figure in this passage, what would you want to say to your children to lead them down a wise path and into the heart of God? If you aren't a parent, what wisdom have you learned that you can pass along to the next generation?*

- *Spend some time considering your own instructions—
  then write them down and share them in love with those
  entrusted to your care.*

Wisdom's Feast, a Table for Fools

Proverbs 9 presents us with a contrast between wisdom and folly that is illustrated in a choice between two banquets at two houses: the seven-pillar palace of Lady Wisdom (vv. 1–12) and the simple home of Foolish (vv. 13–18). While Lady Wisdom gets most of the attention, the "spirit named Foolish" is not ignored. She is a rival to Lady Wisdom, seducing people into a path of destruction explicitly through sexual sin and implicitly through pure foolishness. Of course, the heart of God for our lives is on the side of wisdom: "The starting point for acquiring wisdom is to be consumed with awe as you worship Yahweh" (v.10). The result of diving deep into the heart of God is that "Wisdom will extend your life, making every year more fruitful than the one before" (v.11). Although both houses and ways of life offer an invitation, only one offers a banquet of bread, meat, and wine, with the other providing stolen bread and water.[25] Put more baldly: only one leads to life; the other to hell itself!

- *Make a chart of Lady Wisdom and Foolish, comparing and contrasting the "food" offered at each banquet and what each promises as a result.*

 EXPERIENCE GOD'S HEART

- *Consider which banquet you're attending, which house you're sitting in on a regular basis. Is it Lady Wisdom's party or Foolish's feast? What from the heart of God have you experienced with that attendance? What have you missed out on?*

Wisdom's Treat

What is your go-to treat, either for comfort when life goes sour or as a reward when you've scored a good day? For some, a salty bag of potato chips does wonders. Others run to a chocolate bar or something similarly silky sweet. Then there are those who throw a slab of beef on the grill and smother it with onions and gravy to close out the day.

For the ancient Near East, honey was the delectable treat of the day, the kind straight from the honeycomb. But honey also has medicinal properties that not only soothe the soul but also heal the body. These properties make it the perfect analogy to extol the benefits of running after wisdom in the same way we run after treats for comfort and reward.

- *How does Proverbs 24:13–14 compare honey to wisdom? What does it advise, and why do you suppose it offers such an exhortation?*

- *Does your own attitude concerning God's wisdom reflect Proverbs 24? Explain.*

Don't Be a Fool—or Give In to One

One of the hardest things we can do is walk away from a fool. Something within us wants to set them straight and prove we're right or show them why their path is destructive and will lead to nowhere fast. Yet consider the wisdom of the early church father Ambrose, whose commentary on Proverbs 26:4 offers apt insight: "Your flight is a good one if you do not answer the fool according to his folly. Your flight is good if you direct your footsteps away from the countenance of fools. Indeed, one swiftly goes astray with bad guides; but if you wish your flight to be a good one, remove your ways far from their words."[26]

- *Read 26:4. What do you suppose the author is trying to help us understand about engaging foolish people? And how does Ambrose's commentary enhance these wise words?*

Where Wisdom Resides

If the number of reviews for *The Daily Stoic* daily reader are any indication, clocking in at over eleven thousand just on Amazon alone, people are thirsting for what it takes to live a wise life. Yet people are searching for this knowledge in all the wrong places. We know that Yahweh is the starting place for wisdom, and a proper reverential awe of him should be our manner of life if we hope to discover wisdom and enjoy its benefits. He is not only the source of wisdom, but he is also wisdom itself! Any other source just ends in foolishness. Remember: "If anyone longs to be wise, ask God for wisdom and he will give it!" (James 1:5).

Talking It Out

1. Consider on a scale of 1 to 10 how valuable wisdom is to you right now. Explain your answer. How might that score be influencing the course of your life?

2. Where would you say you are mostly seeking wisdom? How might that source impact the fruit of that wisdom?

3. Describe a time in your life when you trusted the Lord's wisdom completely. What was that like? What was the outcome? What about the reverse, when you thought you knew it all and relied on your head instead of the heart of God for guidance? What happened?

4. Proverbs recognizes that assembling a counsel of trusted voices and heeding their advice is a way into wisdom. Read the following proverbs and list what they teach about seeking counsel and heeding advice: Proverbs 11:14, 12:15, 15:22, 15:32, 18:1, 19:20, 20:18, and 23:23. How can advisers, counselors, or others offer safety in numbers?

LESSON 4

Righteousness vs. Wickedness

If there is one basic truism about all societies, it's that they are often divided into either-or binary categories. Whether in sports rivalries or rival technologies, fast food preferences or political parties, one group is often pitted against another group to create a contrast or sometimes a conflict.

Of course, there's the obvious: Republican versus Democrat; conservatives and liberals. For the longest time, from the mid-90s to the mid-2000s at least, Mac users were pitted against PC users; now it seems to be iOS versus Android. In the land of fast food, it's McDonalds versus Burger King, KFC versus Popeyes, Chipotle versus Qdoba. Then there are the perennial rivalries between Ford owners and Chevy owners, Michigan fans against The Ohio State Buckeyes, Tom Brady versus everyone else.

Lately, there has been much talk about the oppressed versus the oppressor, taking cues from Neo-Marxist ideology that saw a perpetual economic conflict between the haves and have-nots and then sought to turn the tables in favor of the less fortunate. Others now see a perpetual power imbalance between various identity groups (or the identity group *de jure*, as the case may be), insisting said out-group—whoever that might be, for whatever reason—deserves a special hearing and special treatment to atone for past wrongs.

The same sorts of binary structures exist in Scripture as well but not in the way you might think. How does the Bible divide the world? Although you will certainly find the rich and poor discussed, especially in the book of Proverbs, and other such groups as wise and foolish (think Jesus' parable about two house builders at the end of the Sermon on the Mount), there is an overarching division that transcends even those contrasts.

The main biblical fault line is the *righteous* versus the *wicked*. Of course, you don't have to be from any particular nation or support any particular sports team or belong to any particular in-out group to be found in either of these categories. Men and women are righteous and wicked alike. There are plenty of examples of the righteous rich as much as the wicked rich. Same for the poor; there are wicked poor people as well as the righteous poor.

We can't seem to escape such binary rivalries, whether in the world or in Scripture. Yet one set stands above them all, which Proverbs explores and we should grasp with Spirit-filled understanding.

The Fear of the Lord
Is the Beginning of Righteousness

Recall that "We cross the threshold of true knowledge when we live in obedient devotion to God" (Proverbs 1:7). Given this, let's consider what Proverbs tells us about the righteous and the wicked.

- *What do righteousness and wickedness mean? Feel free to use a Bible dictionary or a website like www. biblestudytools.com but also give an initial definition from what you already understand.*

- *Now how do you suppose a proper mindset before God, living in obedient devotion to him with healthy fear, leads to the righteous life? Why does awe-filled worship orient our heart around righteousness?*

- *Consider the opposite, when we refuse to worship Yahweh in awe and reverential fear. How does this choice lead to a life of wickedness? Why is refusing to fear God and worship him in awe the path of the wicked?*

Wise Righteous, Wicked Fools

Solomon believed there are basically two kinds of people in the world: the wise righteous and the wicked fools. We find in Proverbs a strong connection between the last lesson and this one: The wise person possesses God's revelation-knowledge and living-understanding, which translates into a life of righteousness. This God-lover is just and peaceful, blameless and good, trustworthy and kind.

The wicked fool, however, is different altogether. He is greedy and deceitful, violent and cruel, and he speaks only what is perverse. It's no wonder "the Lord detests the lifestyle of the wicked" (15:9). The foolish person is described as being gullible, an idiot, self-sufficient, a mocker, lazy, senseless, and one who rejects revelation-knowledge and living-understanding.

Many of Solomon's wise sayings relate to these two kinds of people, teaching us how to avoid being a wicked fool and instead live as God intends us to live, as his wise, righteous lovers.

- *Proverbs 2:7–15 first makes this connection explicit between wisdom and righteousness. What do we discover?*

- *Why do you suppose wisdom is a necessary starting place for righteous living? In what way are foolishness and wickedness connected?*

Stay on the Right(eous) Path

Proverbs 4:10–27 speaks of two paths: the righteous path and the way of the wicked. This instruction comes after the father's recollection of wisdom's benefits. Here he paints in stark, contrasting colors the two choices laid before a person. "Path" and "way" are used to present two clear avenues down which a person may travel: the well-lit path of righteousness versus the darkened way of the wicked.

- *Most of the fruits from these paths and ways are explored in the rest of this study. Make a list of the contrasts between the path of righteous truth and the way of darkened wickedness. For example, love versus hate. What other fruits come from these two ways, including others not explored in this study?*

- *According to this passage, what qualities or characteristics mark each of these separate ways?*

ℏ WORD WEALTH

When it comes to staying on the right(eous) path, Proverbs 4:23 exhorts, "Above all, guard the affections of your heart, for they affect all that you are." "The Hebrew word *levav* is the most common word for 'heart,' which concerns the inner part of our self. It includes our thoughts, our will, our discernment, and our affections."[27]

- *How might our "heart" play a role in the particular path we take, whether traveling along the way of righteousness or wickedness? In what ways have you noticed how your inner self affects the way you go? Explain.*

- *Proverbs exhorts us to "guard" our inner self, the seat of our will, emotions, thoughts, and affections. It's the word shamar, which carries with it the idea of guarding from danger, preserving, and watching. Why might taking such actions be a crucial step in maintaining our journey on the right life-path? What steps can you take to "Pay attention to the welfare of your innermost being" (v. 23)?*

God Sees Everything

Proverbs 5:21 makes something plain about the way of the righteous and wicked: "God sees everything you do and his eyes are wide open as he observes every single habit you have." This verse comes in the context of the wise father questioning why his son would "be exhilarated by an adulteress—by embracing a woman who is not yours?" (v. 20). It gets at a larger principle that God sees how we live, whether walking the path of righteousness or in the way of the wicked.

Proverbs 15:3 highlights this same principle of Yahweh's all-seeing eyes: "The eyes of the Lord are everywhere and he takes note of everything that happens. He watches over his lovers, and he also sees the wickedness of the wicked." There is a clear moral quality to the Lord's gaze, distinguishing between the two people we have been contrasting, the righteous and wicked. His gaze is a judging gaze.

- *Why is this important to remember when we examine our own way, discerning if we are walking in righteousness or wickedness? How should this knowledge that the Lord sees all we do impact how we walk?*

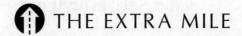# THE EXTRA MILE

There are several passages in Scripture that speak to this principle of Yahweh's all-seeing eye. Read them and explain how each of them informs this passage in Proverbs but also this lesson on the contrast between the righteous and wicked.

Psalm 119:168

Jeremiah 29:23

Jeremiah 32:19

Hebrews 4:13

Life Lessons of the Wicked

Solomon begins Proverbs 6:12–19 in this way: "Here's another life lesson to learn from observing wayward and wicked men" (v. 12). He then outlines how such individuals live on the darkened path of destruction.

- *Read this section, then list the ways of the wayward and wicked person.*

- *How have you witnessed these ways played out, perhaps even in your own life?*

 WORD WEALTH

"The Hebrew word translated 'wayward and wicked man' is actually 'a man of Belial.' This is a metaphor for a worthless man who worships other gods. The name Belial is found in numerous Dead Sea scrolls as a term for Satan."[28] In Lesson 2, we explored how maintaining a posture of awe-filled worship or "fear of the

Lord" lies at the foundation of each of the contrasts presented in this study. The Hebrew makes plain that the ones who walk in the wicked way are not those who fear the Lord but those who worship other gods; they are people of Satan.

- *How do you suppose lawlessness and wickedness are connected to a life oriented around Satan, even his worship?*

This passage on the life lessons of the wicked ends with a list of seven things God hates about this path. "The number seven is the number of fullness and completion. The poetic form here is stating that evil in its fullness is an abomination to God. The seven things are a description of the sin of man that stands in the temple of our bodies attempting to usurp God."[29]

Venerable Bede, an eighth-century English Benedictine monk, offers some intriguing insight into these "capital crimes" committed on the wicked way, suggesting stirring up strife and discord is the worst of the seven:

> The six capital crimes enumerated here
> are nevertheless like minor faults when
> compared with the sowing of discord,
> since the deed that fractures the unity
> and fraternity which were achieved by
> the grace of the Holy Spirit is surely a
> greater sin. For anyone can raise his eyes
> boastfully, lie with the tongue, pollute

himself with murder, plot to harm his neighbor, subject his members to other offenses, and give false testimony against another...Each reprobate, I say, can bring evil upon himself or upon others yet without harming the peace of the church. But what [heretics] do is more serious, who destroy the harmony of fraternal unity by sowing discord.[30]

• *What do you make of Bede's observation that the first six are not as bad as the final one presented in 6:19? Do you agree or disagree, and why might those "who destroy the harmony of fraternal unity by sowing discord" be worse than others?*

The Journey and Destination

Although Ralph Waldo Emerson's oft-quoted maxim "Life is a journey, not a destination" is true to some extent, we know there is an ultimate, eternal end that every person will face. This means the way we live and where we end up are both important; righteous living and a righteous destination are crucial.

- *Proverbs 10:6–31 offers a remarkable overview of righteous wisdom for our journey toward our final, eternal end. Compare and contrast the kind of journey the righteous one and wicked one experience, listing specific traits found in this section.*

🛣 THE EXTRA MILE

"The wicked are blown away by every stormy wind," Proverbs 10:25 warns. "But when a catastrophe comes, the lovers of God have a secure anchor." John Chrysostom, the fourth-century bishop of Constantinople, offers an important observation: "Notice how safe righteousness is: the righteous are saved when they avoid evil, are on the defensive and stand firm constantly. The wicked, on the other hand, are thrown to the ground even when the disturbance or temptation has not attacked completely. Therefore, those who ignore the just judgment of God easily sin."[31]

Both this verse in Proverbs and Chrysostom's comments are reminiscent of the same warning Jesus offered at the end of his Sermon on the Mount, presenting the wise and foolish builders as exemplars of righteous and wicked people.

- *Read Matthew 7:24–27. How might Jesus' words on the day of catastrophe inform what we read in Proverbs 10:25, especially when it comes to our final end?*

- *How does his parable connect to the wise righteous way and foolish wicked way?*

Synergistic Righteousness

Proverbs 11:5–11 returns us to the two-path theology that marks this Wisdom Literature: the righteous are walking on straight paths leading to victory; the wicked walk on a destructive way. In previous verses, such as 3:6, it is clear that the Lord himself is the One who makes our paths straight when we walk in righteous submission.

However, here "we learn that it is a synergistic effort because the behavior of the wise (here referred to as 'the innocent' [or 'good character']) apparently makes one's life easier."[32] As with everything in the book of Proverbs, a life rooted in awe-filled worship in submission to Yahweh will naturally result in righteous fruit.

- *Reread Proverbs 3:6 and 11:5. How do you suppose this synergy plays itself out in the life of the believer?*

- *Paul says something similar in Philippians 2:12, "Now you must continue to make this new life fully manifested as you live in the holy awe of God—which brings you trembling into his presence." How should this verse inform our understanding of walking in the righteous way?*

🂠 EXPERIENCE GOD'S HEART

Paul's full point in Philippians 2 is "Now you must continue to make this new life fully manifested as you live in the holy awe of God—which brings you trembling into his presence. God will continually revitalize you, implanting within you the passion to do what pleases him" (vv. 12–13). There is a principle here that our new, righteous life in Christ is made manifest when we choose to live in response to our experience with the heart of God while also letting the fullness of that heart guide our will and revitalize our actions in a way that pleases him.

- *In your experience with God's heart, do you continue to make his life fully manifested in your life while also letting him tune your heart to his own? How are you living in response to that experience? How are you at letting that heart guide you in all your righteous ways? Explain.*

- *How should this passage, combined with the ones from Proverbs, inform our understanding of walking in the righteous way as we experience God's heart of love and glory?*

The Right Path for Loving Others

God cares not just for those who love him but also for those who don't. And he wants his children to live his way and love him so they can become winsome to others, showing them life choices and a maturing character that they find attractive.

♥ SHARE GOD'S HEART

So one of the reasons it is right to live for God is because it is right for others, for loving them and sharing the heart of God. This is especially true of the way we talk to others. Bible teacher Warren Wiersbe offers some incredible insight into the way we use our tongue, drawing insight from Proverbs 12:

> God uses the mouth of the righteous to bring deliverance (v. 6), but the mouth of the wicked brings bondage (v. 13). Right words must begin with right thoughts (v. 5) and a love for learning (v. 1), and this is where the ungodly person fails. Right words bring good to others and also to those who speak them (v. 14). With your words, you can help to heal those who have been hurt (v. 18) and who have suffered because of lies (vv. 19–22). You can bring joy to those who are depressed and worried (v. 25). Be alert today for God-given opportunities to speak healing words to hurting people.[33]

- *According to Proverbs 12, in what ways do the righteous and wicked use their words? Make a list here.*

- *Now, in what ways do you use your words? List them here.*

- *Are there any changes you need to make with the words you choose to use? If so, what are they?*

Righteous Protection

Proverbs 13:6 promises, "Righteousness is like a shield of protection, guarding those who keep their integrity, but sin is the downfall of the wicked." Here is another instance of Proverbs' two-path theology, where the righteous wise are contrasted with the wicked fools. Something else is added to this contrast:

"protection" versus "downfall," two significant words that reveal the end result of how we live, whether righteously or wickedly.

One example where righteousness protects us is found in verse 10. Furthering the connection with wisdom, we find, "Wisdom opens your heart to receive wise counsel, but pride closes your ears to advice and gives birth to only quarrels and strife." The sinful pride of the wicked leads to destructive quarrels, where the righteous wise open their hearts up to advice, protecting them like a shield.

- *What other ways does righteousness and the fruit of righteous living protect us like a shield? How is the opposite true, where sin and wickedness leads to destruction, our "downfall"?*

The Best Path

Like the book of Proverbs, the Psalms are largely defined by the righteous-wicked dichotomy as well. In Psalm 1, the psalmist pits "the one who follows God's ways" (1:1), the righteous, against the wicked, who "are like chaff blown away by the wind" (1:4). In the end, "The Lord embraces [the righteous'] paths as they move forward while the way of the wicked leads only to doom" (1:6). Which path are you walking?

Talking It Out

1. The book of Proverbs, as well as the rest of the Bible, outlines two kinds of people: righteous and wicked. The Bible frequently portrays these people as "ways" or "paths" to walk along, paving the way for our journey through life. How do you suppose each path looks practically in the day-to-day? Describe each way so you can identify how each path looks.

2. The two-path theology of Proverbs is more than academic lingo for righteous and wicked ways; it's intensely practical. Whom do you know, from your personal life or history, who might serve as an example of both paths? What have they done, and why do they exemplify either of them?

3. What does it mean to you that the Lord sees everything we do, that he takes note of how we are walking, whether in the way of righteousness or wickedness? How are you walking? How are you living? Explain.

4. Consider your tongue: Do you use your words to "soothe and heal" (12:18) and "restore joy to the heart" (v. 25) or "ambush and accuse" (v. 6) as the wicked do? How might this lesson inform and shape how you share the heart of God this week?

LESSON 5

Truth vs. Deceit

"The Boy Who Cried Wolf" is perhaps one of the most beloved and well-known of the Aesop's fables. As the story goes:

> A Shepherd-boy, who watched a flock of sheep near a village, brought out the villagers three or four times by crying out, "Wolf! Wolf!" and when his neighbors came to help him, laughed at them for their pains. The Wolf, however, did truly come at last. The Shepherd-boy, now really alarmed, shouted in an agony of terror: "Pray, do come and help me; the Wolf is killing the sheep!" But no one paid any heed to his cries, nor rendered any assistance. The Wolf, having no cause of fear, at his leisure lacerated and destroyed the whole flock.[34]

The moral of the story? "There is no believing a liar, even when he speaks the truth."

Our world could take notes from this fable! Whether fake news or alternative facts, conspiracy theories about mysterious shadow entities' interference or the latest internet cult sensations peddling the ravings of some anonymous Q fellow—lies rule the day, truth is hard to come by, and there seems to be no wisdom to right the ship. A casual glance at any of the major social media platforms offers Exhibits A through Z.

Except, of course, we have been gifted the light of God's revelation to guide our way. The book of Proverbs is chock-full of his insights. And what it has to share blows Aesop out of the water. For not only does it uncover the consequences of deceit, but it also sheds light on the blessings of truth-telling. We need to understand both as we navigate this post-truth world.

The Fear of the Lord
Is the Beginning of Truth

Let's consider why our heart's condition matters when it comes to truth and deceit.

- *What do truth and deception mean? Feel free to use a Bible dictionary or a website like www.biblestudytools. com but also give an initial definition from what you already understand.*

- *Now how do you suppose a proper attitude before God, living in obedient devotion to him with healthy fear, leads to a life of truth-telling? Why does awe-filled worship orient our heart around the truth?*

- *Consider the opposite, when we refuse to worship Yahweh in awe and reverential fear. How does this choice lead to a life of deception? Why is refusing to fear God and worship him in awe the path of liars?*

Hold on to Truth

"Hold on to loyal love and don't let go," exhorts Proverbs 3:3, "and be faithful to all that you've been taught. Let your life be shaped by integrity, with truth written upon your heart." This verse is part of a set of admonitions using words that often describe Yahweh's own actions and characteristics. In this verse, *hesed* (loyal love) and *'emet* (truth) are two qualities of God we are called to emulate.

The writer implores us to not leave behind loving-kindness and truth, to "bind them around your neck and write them on the tablets of your heart," as it literally reads. This notion of "binding" and "writing" is connected to the law elsewhere in the Hebrew Scriptures (Deuteronomy 6:4–9), where one is encouraged to internalize it so that it guides our actions and purifies our motives. These were the same, the cornerstone creed of Israel.

  • *Why might both loyal love and truth be paired together*
  in this exhortation? How does one lead to the other? Why
  is it important to have both of them bound and written
  upon us?

 SHARE GOD'S HEART

In many ways, the exhortation to loyal love and truth mirrors Jesus' own character, who was "overflowing with tender mercy and truth" (John 1:14). Our world needs people filled with tender mercy and grace, with truth written on our hearts and faithfulness to what we've been taught. Consider those truths that have been written on our heart concerning a whole range of things—from Jesus' divinity to his humanity, from marriage to gender, from political allegiances to human dignity.

- *What are the things we have been taught from the Word of God that we need to hold on to with faithfulness? How should we marry God's own character of loyal love, tender mercies, and grace to what we have been taught and is written on our hearts, especially when it comes to standing for truth in our world?*

🅝 WORD WEALTH

The Hebrew word *'emet* is translated as "truth" here, but it can also be translated as "reliability, sureness; stability, continuance; faithfulness, reliableness."[35] Again, these Hebrew words are often found together, describing God's heart toward those he's covenanted with, attitudes we ourselves are to manifest with one another.

- *First, how does it amplify the meaning of this verse to know that the original Hebrew word for "truth" can also be translated as "reliability" and "faithfulness"?*

- *Now, read the following passages where these two Hebrew words—loyal love and truth—are found together: Exodus 34:6, Psalm 86:15, 108:4, 115:1, and 117:2. What do you learn about these words, and how should your own life be guided by them?*

God Hates Lying

Read Proverbs 6:16–19. Then read it again. For in it, God opens up part of his heart to us, revealing "six evils God truly hates and a seventh that is an abomination to him" (v. 16). Hate is a strong word, but it's true: "The seven items listed are detestable to Yahweh; that is, they are abominations (*to'ebah*) that provoke loathing...Often named in covenantal contexts, abominations were morally offensive."[36]

 EXPERIENCE GOD'S HEART

- *List the six things that God hates. What are your impressions of this list? What does it reveal about the heart of God?*

- *Does it surprise you to find lying on this list? Explain. What does it tell you about truth-telling and deceit that it is on a short list of things God hates?*

- *Why do you suppose God hates lying so much?*

- *How should God's view of lying shape our view and behavior?*

The Power of the Tongue

One of the deeper aspects of this topic of truth and lies in the book of Proverbs is the power of the tongue. Longman explains,

"In Proverbs, the 'tongue' of the righteous (or some other word for speech) is often paired with 'heart.' The idea seems to be that words can reflect what is going on inside, and here the heart stands for one's core personality or character."[37] Since what is in the heart comes out of the mouth, and we truth-tell and deceive with this organ, it's important to ask the Holy Spirit to help us understand the full scope of its power.

- *Read Proverbs 10:18–21 and then 18:20–21. How does Proverbs describe the power of the tongue? How does this power and these verses relate to this topic of truth-telling?*

- *The rest of the Bible has some powerful things to say about the tongue as well, especially James 3:3–12. Read this passage, then connect its perceptions to the wisdom the writer of Proverbs offers in these two previously mentioned passages.*

- *Jesus offers some equally important insight into the power of the tongue, particularly Matthew 15:1–20. Read this passage as well, explaining how his teachings on what comes out of the mouth amplify and extend the wisdom found in Proverbs 10:18–21 and 18:20–21 as well as in James 3:3–12.*

Deceitful Gossipers

Proverbs offers a great deal of wisdom about gossipers, going so far as to warn us to "stay away from people who can't keep their mouths shut" (20:19), not even associating with them. Ross explains why, referencing this proverb:

> It is dangerous to associate with a gossip. The first line pictures the gossip as one who goes about revealing secrets, and the second line warns against associating with the person who talks too much. If a person is willing to talk to you about others, he will be willing to talk to others about you... these people are not necessarily malicious; they just lack discernment and are too garrulous. The less contact one has with a gossip, the better off one will be.[38]

The reason why should be clear from several passages from Proverbs.

- *Read the following verses from Proverbs and make notes about what they tell us about gossipers and the connection between gossip and deception.*

  11:13

  12:13

  18:8

- *How are truth-tellers an antidote to deceitful gossipers?*

Truth-Telling in Business

One of the most difficult areas in which to tell the truth is the marketplace, whether it's as a business owner or manager or as an employee responsible for managing products and budgets. And yet, Proverbs makes it incredibly clear that "Dishonest business practice is something that Yahweh truly hates" (11:1). On the other hand, the passage adds that "it pleases him when we apply the right standards of measurement." Showing it delights God's heart when we're honest in our business dealings.

- *What does it tell you about the heart of God that he cares about how we conduct our business, whether as owners or workers? Who do dishonest business practices affect and how? How does truth-telling impact our work, and who does it affect?*

- *There are several other Proverbs that give specific instruction for business owners and people who work. Read a few of those passages below, then note what you learn:*

    16:11

    20:10

20:23

21:6

Time Will Tell

"Truthful words will stand the test of time, but one day every lie will be seen for what it is" (12:19). Sound familiar? Pretty well summarizes the lesson explored earlier in "The Boy Who Cried Wolf." In time, the value of people's words will be weighed and exposed for what they are: either truth or lies.

- *Jesus says something similar in Luke 8:17, teaching that every hidden thing will eventually "be unveiled and out in the open, made known by the revelation-light." What do you suppose Jesus means here, and how does his teaching amplify this nugget of wisdom found in Proverbs 12?*

- *How should the above proverb, combined with the teachings of Jesus in Luke 8, guide your words? Do you think time has weighed your words well? Explain.*

Truth-Telling Benefits

Wisdom Literature, like the book of Proverbs, functions in two ways: as a beacon of guidance, pointing to the way of righteousness; and as a road sign, signaling the path of wise living. There is both a spiritual, godly dimension, as well as a practical, beneficial dimension for those who are trained by Proverbs.

Not only is truth-telling the godly, righteous thing to do, it also reflects the heart of God himself. It's also the *wise* thing to do, carrying with it practical benefits for those who tell the truth as well as those to whom truth is told. Below are a number of verses that describe these benefits.

- *Read the following proverbs, and note the benefit for righteousness and practical living:*

    13:14

    13:17

    14:25

    20:15

- *When was a time when it was hard to tell the truth but you reaped benefits from committing to the path of truth-telling? What happened, and what was that like?*

Deceitful Consequences

In the previous question, we noted how Wisdom Literature signals the way of righteousness and that it also offers practical benefits to those who are trained by it. The converse is true as well: folly follows those who shun Proverbs' wisdom, leading them down the path of wickedness and into a whole mess of practical consequences.

- *Deceitful living is foolish living, with disastrous consequences. Read the following proverbs. What do they tell us about the consequences of lying and deceiving?*

    19:9

    19:5

20:17

25:18

26:18–19

- *Have you experienced the consequences of lying and deceit? If so, what was that like, and how might you have acted differently?*

God Knows Our Words, and He Cares

One of the most insidious aspects of any sin is the belief that God doesn't see what we do in secret. Because deception is one of those areas that is often done in secret without anyone finding out what we've done, we can con ourselves into believing that we've gotten away with our lie scot-free.

Proverbs 22:12 tells a different story: "God passionately watches over his deep reservoir of revelation-knowledge, but he subverts the lies of those who pervert the truth." Plainly put: Yahweh cares deeply about the truth—going so far as to *natzar* it, the Hebrew word for not only "watches over" but also "guard from danger, preserve" and "keeping with fidelity and faithfulness."

In the last lesson, we saw this principle in Proverbs 15:3, where "The eyes of the Lord are everywhere and he takes note of everything that happens." This passage in 22:12 relates it specifically to Yahweh guarding and preserving knowledge and truth, while also doing something about the deception of liars.

- *What sort of revelation-knowledge and truth do you believe God passionately watches over? How do you suppose he himself subverts the lies of those who pervert such truth?*

- *What does it mean for our acts of truth-telling and deception alike that God knows and sees these acts? How should this realization guide our words?*

A Truth-Teller's Prayer

Every committed follower of Christ should long to be a truth-teller. Our lives should not only center around *the* truth, our loving Savior, but we should make Jesus' teachings on the matter our goal: "A simple 'Yes' or 'No' will suffice. Anything beyond this springs from a deceiver" (Matthew 5:37). But how, when we are tempted to fudge our sales numbers to make our earnings look better, when telling a "white lie" seems right at the time, when holding back what is true about faith and life is easier than telling it like God says it is?

We follow Jesus' teachings about truth-telling and heed the Proverbs' warnings by willing ourselves to tell the truth but also by praying that the Lord will cultivate it within us. Although the Lord calls on us to "continue to make this new life fully manifested as you live in the holy awe of God," we also have the blessed assurance that he "will continually revitalize you, implanting within you the passion to do what pleases him" (Philippians 2:12–13). The Holy Spirit works within you to tell the truth, and the writer of Proverbs gives us the words we can offer up asking him to do that through the truth-teller's prayer:

> God, there are two things I'm asking you
> for before I die, only two:
> Empty out of my heart everything that is
> false—
> > every lie, and every crooked thing.
> > And give me neither undue poverty nor
> undue wealth—
> > but rather, feed my soul with the
> measure of prosperity
> > that pleases you.
> May my satisfaction be found in you.
> > Don't let me be so rich that I don't need
> you
> > or so poor that I have to resort to

dishonesty
　　just to make ends meet.
　　Then my life will never detract from
bringing glory to your name. (Proverbs
30:7–9)

• *Take a moment to pray this prayer now, asking the Lord
to empty your heart of every lie.*

• *What does it tell you about this prayer that the writer
combines both truth-telling and practical provision into
the same prayer?*

The Life of Truth

Aesop is right: "There is no believing a liar, even when he
speaks the truth." Yet the writer of Proverbs offers so much
more than this moral aphorism. For what we find in this divinely
inspired book is not merely a warning against lying; with truth at

the center, we find encouragement for a way of life that fears the Lord and walks in his righteousness. As with all the wisdom in Proverbs, this dual posture is crucial for truth-telling and avoiding lying. For both divine awe and godly righteousness are the only antidotes to a deceitful life.

Talking It Out

1. What is your relationship with the truth? Do you tend to shade it, allowing deception to creep into your words? Or do you let your yes be yes and no be no?

2. Do you struggle with gossip? How might it look in your own life to commit to the path of truth-telling and shun the way of gossipers?

3. Have you been on the receiving end of gossip? If so, what was that like? How did it affect you and your reputation?

4. When was a time that you lied and it turned out badly? What was that like, and what happened?

5. Have you ever witnessed what Proverbs 11:1 condemns: dishonest business practices, perhaps at work or at a store? If so, what was that like? Did you speak up against them, and what was the outcome?

LESSON 6

Humility vs. Pride

Perhaps there is no more familiar proverb than the one found in chapter 16, verse 18: Pride goes before a fall. Or as The Passion Translation phrases it, "Your boast becomes a prophecy of a future failure. The higher you lift yourself up in pride, the harder you'll fall in disgrace." But what is pride?

The main Hebrew word is *ga'on*, which carries with it the idea of "exultation" since its root is the verbal form for "rise up." In a positive sense, it can mean "majesty" and is often used throughout the Old Testament with reference to the Lord. It is often translated in other ways as "arrogance" and "pomp," clearly a negative meaning. The Greek *kauchoamai* carries with it the same idea of "exult" and "exultation" as the Hebrew, resulting in translations from "boast" to "brag." Again, in a positive way, the apostle Paul "boasts in God" (Romans 5:11); in a negative context, the boast is self-directed.

Both definitions from the original Hebrew and Greek sound about right, don't they, especially in the negative senses? Pride is the exultation, the raising up of one's self—which leads to so much destruction across the human spectrum. Pride gets us into wars, it ends marriages, it fuels greed and rage—all leading us down an empty road. "My way, or the highway!" is pride's anthem. It places the self at the center of one's orbit and demands all relationships, circumstances, decisions, and events realign toward that center.

Humility is far different. The Hebrew *'anawah* explains it as "meekness" and "condescension." The latter especially makes sense because it comes from the verbal root for "to be bowed down." The Greek is *tapeinoō*, which bears the same meaning, "to bring low, to level, to descend." Rather than raising our self up in pride, humility seeks to bow the self low. As Proverbs 22:4 expresses it, "Laying yourself down in tender surrender before the Lord will bring life, prosperity, and honor as your reward."

Instead of raising up the self in exultation, we raise up the Lord with holy awe before us in worship. In doing so, our life becomes about God, not us; it is other-oriented, not self-oriented. And this life comes with the reward of "life, prosperity, and honor."

The Fear of the Lord
Is the Beginning of Humility

As we have seen throughout this study, wise living starts with a proper posture of awe-filled worship and fear of the Lord. Pride can get in the way of that, and its antidote is humility. Let's turn now to see what insight we can gain about pride and humility.

- *What do humility and pride mean? Feel free to use a Bible dictionary or a website like www.biblestudytools. com but also give an initial definition from what you already understand.*

- *Now how do you suppose a proper life orientation before God, living in obedient devotion to him with healthy fear, leads to a humble life? Why does awe-filled worship orient our heart around humility?*

- *Consider the opposite, when we refuse to worship Yahweh in awe and reverential fear. How does this orientation lead to a pride-filled life? Why is refusing to fear God and worship him in awe the path of pride?*

God Hates Pride

In the previous lesson, we examined Proverbs 6:16–19, noting the list of seven things "God truly hates," including: a lying, deceitful tongue; shedding innocent blood; a heart that schemes wickedness; feet that run swiftly toward evil; a false witness; and someone who stirs up strife.

Among this list is "Putting others down while considering yourself superior." This is what it means to be prideful, to be *haughty*, carrying with it the idea of highness, entitlement, exultation—which is another Hebrew word used here, *rum*. In fact, prideful consideration of superiority makes the top of the list; pride is the first thing that God hates!

• *Does it surprise you to find pride on this list of things God hates? Why do you suppose God hates a haughty, prideful spirit so much?*

• *What do you think about such a spirit of superiority and pride when you see it in others and in yourself?*

Haughty House Smash-Down

Frequently in Wisdom Literature, whether in Proverbs or Psalms, the writer will offer insight using contrasting pairs. We have seen that from the beginning of the book, where the wise and foolish are contrasted, along with the righteous and wicked, even ants and the lazy in a few lessons. Here we find two more contrasting pairs: the widow and the haughty. "The Lord champions the widow's cause, but watch him as he smashes down the houses of the haughty!" (Proverbs 15:25).

- *First, what is the widow's cause? By what might it be marked? For example, a humble dependence on others for provision.*

- *Second, the verse envisions the haughty constructing a house, where their life is built upon their pride. How might such a life be constructed? For example, the prideful sense of security from money.*

- *Now, contrast the pair: why do you suppose the Lord is the widow's "champion," while he opposes the haughty—with a smash-down?*

The Predictable Nature of Pride

English preacher Charles Spurgeon highlights a common saying of his time: "coming events cast their shadows before them." The same is true of a haughty, prideful heart, which is a prophetic prelude to the evil that will eventually come. "Pride is as safely the sign of destruction as the change of mercury in the weather-glass is the sign of rain; and far more infallibly so than that. When men have ridden the high horse, destruction has always overtaken them. Let David's aching heart show that there is an eclipse of a man's glory when he dotes upon his own greatness."[39]

To illustrate, Spurgeon directs our attention to Nebuchadnezzar, who was "the mighty builder of Babylon" but was reduced to "creeping on the earth, devouring grass like oxen, until his nails had grown like bird's claws, and his hair like eagle's feathers."[40] In this way, pride reduced the Babylonian boaster to nothing better than a beast.

Spurgeon's point is that Nebuchadnezzar's destruction was predictable because of the predictable nature of pride. "Coming events cast their shadows before them." Whether pride or an impending thunderstorm, the writing is on the wall.

- *Read Proverbs 16:18–19 and 18:12 with the above commentary in mind. How have you seen the principle of these passages illustrated?*

🙂 EXPERIENCE GOD'S HEART

Spurgeon continues this point with a lesson on the heart of God: "God hates high looks, and never fails to bring them down. All the arrows of God are aimed at proud hearts."[41] Hate seems like a strong word to use of the Lord, yet it reflects his holy heart. Because there is not a speck of sin in him, because he is fundamentally holy and every one of his attributes reflect his sin-lessness, he cannot help but hate sin, including the sin of pride.

Therefore, he will bring the haughty down to destruction. Proverbs 16:5 makes this destruction clear: "Yahweh detests all the proud of heart, for pride attracts his punishment—and you can count on that!" In light of this aspect of God's heart and surety of destruction for the prideful, the great preacher offers a strong measure of exhortation for us believers that bears quoting:

> O Christian, is your heart haughty this
> evening?...Are you glorying in your graces
> or your talents? Are you proud of yourself,
> that you have had holy frames and sweet
> experiences? Mark you, reader, there is
> a destruction coming to you also. Your
> flaunting poppies of self-conceit will be
> pulled up by the roots, your mushroom
> graces will wither in the burning heat,

and your self-sufficiency shall become as straw for the dunghill. If we forget to live at the foot of the cross in deepest lowliness of spirit, God will not forget to make us smart under his rod. A destruction will come to you, O unduly exalted believer, the destruction of your joys and of your comforts, though there can be no destruction of your soul.[42]

- *Does your heart reflect the holy humility of Christ, or is your heart haughty and prideful? More pointedly: "Are you glorying in your graces or your talents? Are you proud of yourself, that you have had holy frames and sweet experiences?" Consider those areas of your life that exude pride, writing them down to make them plain.*

- *Take a moment to ask the Holy Spirit to search your heart, revealing any speck of sinful pride within and asking him to dismantle any spirit of haughtiness in you.*

The Way of Humility

Many of the proverbs show what it looks like to live in pride, wearing haughtiness as a badge of honor. In contrast, what is the way of humility? Proverbs 22:4 explains: "Laying your life down in tender surrender before the Lord will bring life, prosperity, and honor as your reward."

- *"Laying your life down in tender surrender" is an explicit act of humility. How might this look in our own life, to live life in complete and humble surrender to the Lord? Give a few specific examples to make the humble life concrete.*

- *Proverbs reveals that when we walk in humility before the Lord, "life, prosperity, and honor" will be our reward. How have you seen this played out in your own life? When have you received the benefits of "life, prosperity, and honor" after walking in humility?*

The best view we have been given into the way of humility is the Son of God himself, when Jesus became one of us, not counting his divinity something to be leveraged to his own advantage, but rather emptying himself in humility and taking on our own likeness.

- *Read Philippians 2:1–11, where Paul exhorts us to consider Christ's example and "Let his mindset become your motivation" (v. 5). From both this passage and the Gospels, list the ways Christ humbled himself.*

Honor, Self-Honor, and the Humble Life

Proverbs is consistently teaching against the dangers of promoting our own status, honor, and power. In other words, self-honor and the pride that accompanies it. Consider Proverbs 25:6–7, which explores a key principle of the humble life:

> Don't boast in the presence of a king
>   or promote yourself by taking a seat at
> the head table
>   and pretending that you're someone
> important.
> For it is better for the king to say to you,
>   "Come, you should sit at the head table,"
>   than for him to say in front of everyone,
>   "Please get up and move—
>   you're sitting in the place of the prince."

The same issue of pride and humility is echoed in Proverbs 29:23, "Lift yourself up with pride and you will soon be brought low, but a meek and humble spirit will add to your honor." Here is another: "It's good to eat sweet things, but you can take too much. It's good to be honored, but to seek words of praise is not honor at all" (25:27).

- *The principle in these verses isn't condemning honor entirely but self-honor. What might be the difference between receiving honor and giving self-honor?*

- *What are the dangers of self-honor—both practically, whether at work or in your community, and spiritually when it comes to your heart?*

DIGGING DEEPER

"Don't claim honor that is not yours to claim" is good advice. In fact, Jesus offers similar advice in Luke 14:1–12, while deepening its meaning. Perhaps this very proverb is the background to Jesus' own words of advice. Here, while he is at the house of a prominent Pharisee, Jesus noticed "the guests for the meal were all vying for the seats of honor" (v. 7). Then he shared a parable.

New Testament scholar David Garland notes:

> This absorption with honor spans cultures and centuries. We may confess in prayer that we are worms of the dust and sing about amazing grace that saves wretches like us, but we love our little distinctions— and from God's perspective they are indeed little. When God's evaluation of our niche in his reign does not match our own assessment of our worth, the consequences will bring far more than shame.[43]

Scrambling to claim honor is our default.

This gets back to the Proverbs instruction that God hates pride, and the way of humility is the way of wisdom—with eternal consequences. Garlands goes on to say that Jesus isn't merely offering advice on how to avoid embarrassment but rather "rejects entirely any desire to bask in the ephemeral admiration of others and uses this meal setting to warn about God's judgment... Self-seeking is ultimately self-defeating, but it is an immutable divine principle that 'God opposes the proud, but shows favor to the humble'"[44]—making Jesus' parable about far more than just proper table etiquette.

- Read Jesus' teaching on the subject of self-honor and humility in Luke 14:1–12. What direct connections are there between Jesus' teaching here in Luke and the Proverbs passage above? How do both address self-honor and humility?

- How does Jesus deepen this wise, humble way by connecting it to God's judgment? What sort of warning should it offer the prideful?

Don't Be a Know-It-All

We've all known the person at work or in our circle of friends, maybe in our Sunday school or small group at church, who could be described as a know-it-all. Whether it's politics or sports, cooking or lawn care, there are those people who are smug, conceited, and convinced they are right. Perhaps there is more danger in Christians who are such people, for they lack the kind of humility that should come with ongoing sanctification in Christ. Proverbs offers a different approach to knowledge, as well as several verses of council for the person who believes they know it all.

- *First, Proverbs explicitly connects acting with presumption, "convinced that you're right," with destructive results ("[falling] flat on your face"), while revealing "humility leads to wisdom" (11:2). Why might know-it-alls be headed for a hard fall, and why is humility a wiser way?*

- *Proverbs 26:12 deepens the point: "There's only one thing worse than a fool, and that's the smug, conceited man always in love with his own opinions." Why do you suppose such a person is worse than a fool?*

❤ SHARE GOD'S HEART

Pride can be an ugly thing. Not only in our own life but also in the heart of others. We've all known those people, the ones who not only think they know it all but also walk around smug, conceited, and in love with their own perspective. It's easy to make a choice to keep our distance or even walk away entirely. Yet sometimes the most loving thing we can do is hold up a mirror to someone and show them their pride, gently pointing out this ugly sin, especially with those we care about. God's heart is a humble heart; he knows that's the best way to live, and he longs for people to share in this wise way.

- *Do you know a know-it-all? If so, what are they like, what's it like to be around them, what do other people say about them? Have they reaped consequences for living with such pride, or are they on the brink?*

- *How might it look this week to pull them aside and lovingly share the gracious heart of God with them by holding up a mirror to their sin?*

- *Before you even consider pointing out someone else's fault, it's always beneficial to consider your own. Are you beset by the know-it-all mentality? How does it display itself in your life? Recognizing and dealing with our own faults helps us be more charitable and compassionate toward those who struggle similarly.*

Like Christ

"Your boast becomes a prophecy of a future failure," Proverbs 16:18 instructs. "The higher you lift yourself up in pride, the harder you'll fall in disgrace." Instead of raising yourself up over others, make it your goal to lower yourself in humility—just like Jesus Christ did. After all, although he was God, "yet he gave no thought to seizing equality with God as his supreme prize," as Paul writes in Philippians 2. "Instead he emptied himself of his outward glory by reducing himself to the form of a lowly servant. He became human! He humbled himself and became vulnerable, choosing to be revealed as a man and was obedient" (vv. 7–8). May Christ's self-humility be our life goal!

Talking It Out

1. On a scale of 1 to 10, how would you rate your own attitude of pride and humility, where 1 is more prideful and 10 is humbler? Explain your rating.

2. In what spheres of life do you find yourself humblest or most prideful? Why? How would you like to grow in this area?

3. When have you witnessed a clear example of pride, whether in your own life or someone else's? What was that like, and how did the situation turn out? Now what about humility, where someone humbled himself or herself or acted with humility? What was striking about this person and his or her behavior?

4. Jesus' example of humility, found in Philippians 2, stands as a clarion call to live life with humility, along with Proverbs' wise words. How might it look in your own life to listen to these words on humility while also letting Christ's mindset and attitude be yours? Offer a specific example or area that you can work on to adopt the way of humility.

LESSON 7

Joy vs. Sorrow

"Find out where joy resides," wrote Scottish poet Robert Louis Stevenson, "and give it a voice far beyond singing. For to miss the joy is to miss all." Good advice, which begs the question: Where does joy reside? Where can you find it, and what is this joy in the first place? The kind that's deep down in your heart and stays long after the high of the moment fades?

It seems every generation asks these sorts of questions, but their answers are more acutely felt in our modern day. Money (and the stuff it buys) is one source of joy—whether clothes or cars, gadgets or gated communities. Drugs and alcohol and sex are others, where intoxicating highs promise to numb away the despair and sorrow of modern existence, as fleeting as those promises are. Accumulating more education and climbing the corporate ladder are ways we make meaning out of our lives and find joy, or at least its twin, happiness. More recently still, others insist that choosing our own identities from a myriad of options and living out of our true selves, however that is defined, will lead to the Holy Grail of joy.

But is this true? Does joy reside in money, pleasure, education, work, and personal meaning-making? If not, then where can we find it, especially to help lead us out of the grief of modern life? The book of Proverbs offers a clue:

If you wait at wisdom's doorway,
     longing to hear a word for every day,
     joy will break forth within you as you
listen for what I'll say.
For the fountain of life pours into you
every time that you find me,
     and this is the secret of growing in the
delight
     and the favor of the Lord. (8:34–35)

Wisdom, the kind that's straight from the heart of God, is what infuses us with joy. It leads to "fountains of life" and blessing. The secret to the kind of deep, inner joy we're all longing for is saturating ourselves in the Lord's wisdom-way. When we do, we receive and grow in "the delight and the favor of the Lord."

The Fear of the Lord Is the Beginning of Joy

Joy and sorrow are facts of life, and they also provide revelation-insight into what is involved in living "in obedient devotion to God" (1:7).

- *What do joy and sorrow mean? Feel free to use a Bible dictionary or a website like www.biblestudytools.com but also give an initial definition from what you already understand.*

- *Now how do you suppose a proper attitude before God, living in obedient devotion to him with healthy fear, leads to a joy-filled life? Why does awe-filled worship orient our heart around joy?*

- *Consider the opposite, when we refuse to worship Yahweh in awe and reverential fear. How does this approach lead to a life of despair? Why is refusing to fear God and worship him in awe the path of sorrow?*

Wisdom's Joy-Filled Blessings

The book of Proverbs is a book of wisdom in which the kind of life God intends for us is explored and explained to guide us into this meaningful life. Proverbs 3:13–18 showcases a sort of hymn-like poem praising what Lady Wisdom offers the world. The poem is bracketed by the dual "Blessings" language, which is a different word than is normally used. Instead of *barakh*, the word is *'ashre*, which carries with it the meaning of "being made happy" alongside being blessed. Although the blessed life is a wise life, it's more than that: wisdom leads to happiness and joy.

Here, the worth and supremacy of wisdom is extolled, leading to a joy-filled life found in this promise: "Blessings pour over the ones who find wisdom, for they have obtained living-understanding" (v. 13). The King James Version translates verse 13 in this way: "Happy is the man that findeth wisdom, and the man that getteth understanding."

- *Why do you suppose wisdom is considered "blessed" and the one who finds such wisdom is considered "happy"—where blessings pour into their life, leading to overflowing joy?*

- *What blessings does this passage touch on that Lady Wisdom unveils to those touched by wisdom? How does Lady Wisdom give us joy and happiness?*

The Source of Joy: Wisdom

The last question explored the reality that the wise person is a happy, joy-filled person. But where is that wisdom found? Where is our happiness found? Some find "happiness" in a bottle or at the tip of a needle. Others in money and accumulating the stuff of American, middle-class suburbia—the two-story house and two-stall garage, the white-picket fence, and 1.9 kids. More recently, culture tells us happiness is found in our identity and living our truth.

Contrasting all of these sources of happiness and joy, the book of Proverbs says otherwise: "So listen, my sons and daughters, to everything I tell you, for nothing will bring you more joy than following my ways...If you wait at wisdom's doorway, longing to hear a word for every day, joy will break forth within you as you listen for what I'll say" (8:32, 34).

- *Read chapter 8 to get the fuller context of this passage. According to these verses, where (and even who) is our source of happiness, delight, and joy? How does this contrast with the sources that our culture points to?*

Consider how this chapter ends and the words of revelation-insight the writer gives to close out chapter 8: "For the fountain of life pours into you every time that you find me, and this is the secret of growing in the delight and the favor of the Lord. But those who stumble and miss me will be sorry they did! For ignoring what I have to say will bring harm to your own soul. Those who hate me are simply flirting with death!" (vv. 35–36). Put plainly, those who listen to the Lord's wise Words find joy and delight; those who don't, reap only despair and destruction.

- *Make a chart with two columns. On one side, list several joy-filled delights brought on by God's wisdom, such as sexual purity and generous giving. On the other, list the grieving fallout that comes from pursuing the opposite, such as sexual addiction and bankruptcy.*

❤ EXPERIENCE GOD'S HEART

There is an active, imperative verb in Proverbs 8:32: "Listen… to everything I [Wisdom, which is from the Lord] tell you." You could also add the word *longing*, for it is the one "longing to hear a word for every day" from the Lord that "joy will break forth within you" (v. 34). This is a call to intentionally experience the very good heart of God through the wisdom he freely gives us. But it takes intention; it takes a certain amount of work to listen to and wonder about, to wait and long for these words of wisdom straight from God's heart with awe-filled worship and holy fear.

* *When it comes to God's wise Word, how intentional are you about listening and longing, waiting and wondering? If joy and happiness are found in the Lord and his wisdom, what is your plan for plumbing its depths in order to find the kind of joy-filled life he intends for you?*

Parents' Joy and Sorrow

We have already seen in previous chapters how the categories of wise and righteous, contrasted with foolish and wicked, are key to the book, especially chapter 10. These contrasted pairs carry with them a number of benefits as well as fallout not only for the one who is wise, who is trained in righteousness—or conversely, the one who is foolish and wicked, but also for those around them, particularly parents.

The wise and righteous bring joy to their parents, not sorrow or grief as the foolish wicked do. Proverbs 10:1 makes this clear, "When wisdom comes to a son, joy comes to a father. When a son turns from wisdom, a mother grieves."

- *It is true that "Parents of a numskull will have many sorrows, for there's nothing about his lifestyle that will make them proud" (17:21). Have you experienced the full measure of this proverb as a parent? If so, what has that been like, how has it made you feel?*

- *Take a moment to journal your thoughts about how your foolish child has brought you grief and sorrow. Then pray over these feelings, asking the Lord to offer you encouragement and wisdom.*

- *Now consider whether and how you may have been foolish during your childhood. Did you bring grief to your parents? If so, have you acknowledged that to your mom and dad and asked for their forgiveness?*

Parenting is not all gloomy sorrow. While our children's foolish actions bring us sorrow, our wise, godly children bring us pride: "When a father observes his child living in godliness, he is ecstatic with joy—nothing makes him prouder!" (23:24)

- *If you are a parent, when have you experienced the truth of this proverb? When have you been most proud of the evidence of your child's godly living?*

- *Similarly, take a moment to journal all the ways your wise, godly child has brought you ecstatic joy in how they have lived—ending your moment with a time of prayer and thanksgiving to the Lord.*

❤ SHARE GOD'S HEART

The truth of Proverbs 17:25 is often very painful for people: "A father grieves over the foolishness of his child, and bitter sorrow fills his mother." Perhaps they've chosen to live and lean into a lifestyle that is contrary to God's Word, bringing deep, bitter sorrow for their parents. Some refuse to work and take responsibility for their financial future, living in their parents' basement and mooching off their goodwill. Others fall into addictions that not only sap their own joy but also the joy of those who are around them.

- *Whom do you know who reflects this proverb? How might you share the comforting heart of God in prayer-filled solidarity with a grieving father or sorrowful mother because of their foolish children?*

- *Take a moment to pray for those fathers and mothers you know are experiencing the full measure of this proverb. Then take the opportunity to encourage them in the next week, reaching out with God's love in a tangible, practical way.*

Choose Cheer, Focus on Joy

Let's face it: life is full of trouble. Some experience it more than others, but we'll all face struggles and sorrow in one form or another—whether financial or relational, work related or family related. Although sometimes we bring trouble on ourselves, quite often the sorrows we bear are out of our control, brought on by the foolishness and sin of others. About the only thing we can control in this life is our reaction to it, how we choose to act in response.

Jeff Bezos, former CEO of Amazon, has often quipped that "complaining isn't a strategy." Meaning: grumbling about changes or problems, whether in business specifically or life generally, will get you nowhere. Choosing to respond positively will. Will our sorrow and struggles make us bitter or better? One way to respond is by choosing joy. Consider these proverbs:

> A cheerful heart puts a smile on your face,
> but a broken heart leads to depression.
> Everything seems to go wrong when you feel
> weak and depressed...But when you choose
> to be cheerful, every day will bring you more
> and more joy and fullness...Eyes that focus
> on what is beautiful bring joy to the heart,
> and hearing a good report refreshes and
> strengthens the inner being. (15:13, 15, 30)

Proverbs acknowledges that a happy heart brings us cheer, but when a heart is weighed down by sorrow, it crushes us.

- *How do you often respond to struggle? With sorrow or joy? Explain. What does the above passage exhort you to do?*

The Joy of Marriage

There is much in this world that brings us joy and happiness. For one, the joy of our salvation, knowing we have been ransomed from death, forgiven of our sins, and adopted into the family of God for eternity. Work also provides a measure of joy, feeling fully alive when we are doing something that we know we were made to do. Friends also infuse us with happiness, whether around the table sharing a meal or on a couch sharing our heart. Perhaps we can receive no greater joy aside from our salvation than marriage and the marriage bed. Read how the book of Proverbs acknowledges both:

> When a man finds a wife, he has found a
> treasure! For she is the gift of God to bring
> him joy and pleasure. (18:22)
> Your sex life will be blessed as you take
> joy and pleasure in the wife of your youth.
> (5:18)

- *In what ways has God designed marriage and sex to give us joy and pleasure? List those ways as well as the sorrow that finds those who violate God's design, both through divorce and adultery.*

- *How have you experienced the truth of these two proverbs, finding joy and pleasure from your marriage and from your spouse?*

Joy, Joy, Joy

There is a catchy children's song you may be familiar with that encourages kids (and kids at heart) to broadcast to the world that they've got the kind of joy Proverbs speaks about:

> I've got the joy, joy, joy, joy
> Down in my heart (where?)
> Down in my heart (where?)
> Down in my heart
> I've got the joy, joy, joy, joy
> Down in my heart (where?)
> Down in my heart to stay[45]

Do you possess this kind of joy? Are you seeking after the kind of joy that is rooted in a wise, righteous life lived in worshipful awe of the Lord? Stevenson is right: "Find out where joy resides." The *true* source of joy. The joy of the Lord that not only transcends sorrow and grief but also snuffs it out of our lives!

Talking It Out

1. In what ways does our culture promote happiness? How does it contrast with the joy of the Lord?

2. Have you run after the happiness of culture? Where did it leave you? What has the Lord's joy meant to you instead?

3. How have you received the happy, joy-filled benefits from a life lived in wisdom?

4. As a child—whether young or adult—have you brought your parents grief or joy? Explain. How might you want the Holy Spirit to work in your life in order to make a change that blesses your parents?

5. Jesus acknowledged, "In this unbelieving world you will experience trouble and sorrows, but you must be courageous, for I have conquered the world!" (John 16:33). Why should this reality that Jesus has conquered the world give us joy? What should be the focus of our heart in light of his conquering?

LESSON 8

Generosity vs. Greed

Money, wealth, the rich. Debt, poverty, the poor.

These contrasts conjure up all sorts of feelings and images and personal connections. Some good, some bad. Some painful, even embarrassing. Regardless, money and how we handle it seems to be a perennial issue that affects us all at some point in our life. Money really does make the world go round, in one way or another. And some of us are just holding on for dear life.

Why is money so problematic? Why are there so many emotions wrapped up in that single word? One illustration is found in the oft-told story about how hunters capture monkeys in India. As the story goes, baskets or jars are filled with peanuts; then they are set beneath trees to lure the wily, wiggly creatures from hiding. Importantly, these baskets and jars are only given a narrow opening at the top. An opening just large enough for our wily, wiggly monkey to stick his arm and reach inside the basket to grab a handful of peanuts. When they do, the hunter simply walks over, grabs the monkey, and stuffs it in his sack!

If our furry creature is so wily and wiggly, why don't they simply scamper away, you ask? Here's the catch: the monkey has grabbed a handful of peanuts, so he cannot remove its arm from the narrow opening in the trap. What's more: the little guy is so intent on keeping those peanuts, he cannot let go. He cannot *not* hold on to his newfound peanut-wealth even with the prospect of being captured.

Sometimes we are so blinded by scarcity—the belief that we lack and have nothing or risk losing something—that we can't see how much we do have, how much abundance we've got, and we risk losing it all. Conversely, we are so fixated on what we do have and obsessed with keeping it that we can't let go—not merely for the sake of giving away what we have to others but also for the sake of saving our souls.

After all, "even if you were to gain all the wealth and power of this world with everything it could offer you—at the cost of your own life—what good would that be?" (Matthew 16:26). Proverbs echoes the same warnings, turning our attention to our relationship with wealth and generosity as well as our relationship to the poor and greedy. Where you find yourself on that spectrum is crucial.

The Fear of the Lord
Is the Beginning of Generosity

- *What do generosity and greed mean? Feel free to use a Bible dictionary or a website like www.biblestudytools. com but also give an initial definition from what you already understand.*

- *Now how do you suppose a proper mindset before God, living in obedient devotion to him with healthy fear, leads to a generous life? Why does awe-filled worship orient our heart around generosity?*

- *Consider the opposite, when we refuse to worship Yahweh in awe and reverential fear. How does this mindset lead to a greedy life? Why is refusing to fear God and worship him in awe the path of greed?*

Generosity Begins with God

From lesson 2, we have seen that wisdom flows from a heart of awe-filled worship; fearing the Lord is the start of wise living. The same is true of generosity. It begins with God, with our posture of generosity toward the Lord himself. Consider Proverbs 3:9–10:

> Glorify God with all your wealth,
>> honoring him with your firstfruits,
>> with every increase that comes to you.
> Then every dimension of your life will
> overflow with blessings
>> from an uncontainable source of inner joy!

This passage speaks of having a proper generosity toward Yahweh, laying at his feet the best of all we have in a spirit of enthusiastic generosity and praise. The "firstfruits" are the best of a crop and are expanded to include a generous outpouring of everything that we receive. The result is a promised prosperity in every dimension of our life, overflowing and uncontainable.

- *Consider your posture toward the Lord with what you have. Do you generously glorify him with your wealth, whether material or otherwise?*

- *People walking in wisdom are generous people. If we are not fearing the Lord with our wealth, honoring him generously, why would we extend generosity to others? How generous, then, are you with the Lord? Do you think this carries over to your level of generosity with others? Explain.*

♥ EXPERIENCE GOD'S HEART

It is a biblical truth that all we own belongs to God; we're just wealth managers. Those firstfruits mentioned in the above Proverbs are straight from the generous heart of God. First Chronicles 29:12 explicitly states that wealth and honor come from the Lord, and our everyday encounter with God's generous heart proves this. Jesus himself reminds us in Matthew 7 that all we have is from this heart of generosity, from food to clothing, so we have nothing to worry about. Our freedom from worry frees us for generosity—"all because God loves hilarious generosity!" as Paul writes in 2 Corinthians 9:7.

- *How have you encountered the generous heart of God? What specifically has God provided for you, and where are the areas where his generosity has overflowed?*

The Benefits of Wholistic Generosity

Proverbs 11:24–25 makes a startling declaration: "Generosity brings prosperity, but withholding from charity brings poverty. Those who live to bless others will have blessings heaped upon them, and the one who pours out his life to pour out blessings will be saturated with favor."

Revealed here is the principle that there are benefits to a life of wholistic generosity, extending beyond material possessions, yes, but also including them. "As God sees that he can trust us to be generous with what he gives us," writes New Testament scholar Craig Blomberg, "and as we become conduits of his blessings, including financial ones, to others, he often gives us still more economic prosperity."[46]

The great English preacher Charles Spurgeon continues this thought, reminding us that generosity isn't just about giving money: "We are here taught the great lesson, that to get, we must give; that to accumulate, we must scatter; that to make ourselves happy, we must make others happy; and that in order to become spiritually vigorous, we must seek the spiritual good of others. In watering others, we are ourselves watered."

Spurgeon goes on to explain how:

> We do not know what tender sympathies
> we possess until we try to dry the widow's
> tears, and soothe the orphan's grief. Oh,
> what gracious lessons some of us have
> learned at sick beds! We went to teach the
> Scriptures, we came away blushing that
> we knew so little of them. In our converse
> with poor saints, we are taught the way
> of God more perfectly for ourselves and
> get a deeper insight into divine truth. So
> that watering others makes us humble. We
> discover how much grace there is where
> we had not looked for it; and how much the

> poor saint may outstrip us in knowledge.
> Our own comfort is also increased by our
> working for others. We endeavor to cheer
> them, and the consolation gladdens our
> own heart.[47]

Spurgeon's point, along with Blomberg's, is that in any number of ways, when we are generous, we receive back just as much as what we give—whether from teaching or comforting, giving money or food.

- *Read Proverbs 11:24–25 again and 22:9, 16, and 28:27. What do these verses teach us about the benefits of generosity?*

 THE EXTRA MILE

Paul reflects this same exhortation in 2 Corinthians 9:6: "A stingy sower will reap a meager harvest, but the one who sows from a generous spirit will reap an abundant harvest." Another way of phrasing this exhortation is from the Aramaic: "'the one who sows with a storehouse of seed' (remaining). This describes a farmer who is stingy with his sowing. Since he has a storehouse of seed, he can afford to sow liberally."[48]

Paul wrote to a wealthy community and encouraged them to give generously to the poor in Jerusalem, sending Titus to take up a collection. In his appeal to generosity, he pointed to the Macedonian Christians, "For even during a season of severe difficulty, tremendous suffering, and extreme poverty, their super-abundant joy overflowed into an act of extravagant generosity" (8:2).

- *How does Paul's instruction to the Church of Corinth reflect the wisdom of generosity found in Proverbs 11:24–25?*

- *Read 2 Corinthians 8–9. Explain how Paul makes his appeal to the Corinthians to live a life of generosity? What can you learn from Paul's exhortation for how you walk in the wisdom of the Lord in this area of life?*

Giving to the Poor Means Giving to God

Whenever we may feel like giving of whatever wealth we have, remember what Proverbs 19:17 teaches: "Every time you give to the poor you make a loan to the Lord. Don't worry—you'll be repaid in full for all the good you've done."

The early church leader Cyril, bishop of Alexandria, offers important commentary that illuminates the meaning of this exhortation to giving:

> The lesson, therefore, which he teaches us
> is love for the poor, which is precious in
> the sight of God. Do you feel pleasure in
> being praised when you have any friends
> or relatives feasting with you? I tell you of
> something far better: angels shall praise
> your bounty, and the rational powers above,
> and holy men as well; and he too shall
> accept it who transcends all, and who loves
> mercy and is kind. Lend to him fearing
> nothing, and you will receive with interest
> whatever you gave, for "he," it says, "who
> has pity on the poor lends unto God."[49]

- *"Lend to him fearing nothing," says Cyril. Do you fear generous giving? If so, why? How should this verse and Cyril's exhortation inform and guide your generosity?*

Give, Don't Crave

Whether it's fast fashion or fast food, trading in the smartphone for the latest upgrade or turning in the keys of your current car for the latest hotrod model—we live in a culture that celebrates the ever-greater accumulation of things in order to satisfy our every craving. Proverbs offers a warning, especially for the lazy, and a way out of greedy, gluttonous cravings:

> Taking the easy way out is the habit of a
> lazy man,
>> and it will be his downfall.
>> All day long he thinks about all the
> things that he craves,
>> for he hasn't learned the secret that the
> generous man has learned:
>> extravagant giving never leads to
> poverty. (21:25–26)

Contrasting the greedy, craving, sluggard is the generous, giving, righteous. Unlike the former, who thinks only about satisfying his own desires, the generous person practices continual giving—and learns an important lesson.

- *The Bible continually condemns both laziness and gluttonous greed. Why do you suppose the two often go together? Why does a lazy person continually crave more, and why will it be his or her downfall?*

- *Why is generous giving both an antidote to laziness and the antithesis of continually craving more? How might it look in your life to focus your energy on being generous precisely in the areas in which you crave more?*

Be Generous to the Poor

The poor have always been looked after by the Lord, his loving heart opening up to them with provision and protection. He made special provisions for them in the law of Moses; the book of Ruth showcases this, with the requirement to let the poor glean certain portions of the field. Jesus said he was sent to preach God's good news to the poor, the poor in every sense of the word. So it is no surprise the Wisdom Literature of Proverbs makes similar exhortations.

Not only do we find "The rich and the poor have one thing in common: the Lord God created each one" (22:2), revealing zero favoritism from God between the two, but we also find several commands from the Lord when it comes serving the poor and being generous toward those who have little. This is no surprise since we are to be generous toward everyone. Dallas Willard explains:

> As we are to honor all human beings (1 Pet. 2:17), so we are to honor the poor. We are to respect them and show them our respect. The distinction between rich and poor is permanently affixed to human life...On the other hand, it always insists that the needy are to be cared for, that the

poor are not to be taken advantage of but
defended, and that they are to be taken
into consideration in all aspects of life.

Willard reminds us that in taking care of the poor, defending
them, and pouring out our generosity upon them, "The overarching command is to love, and the first act of love is always
attention. Therefore, the poor are not to be avoided and forgot-
ten."[50] Instead, they are to be attended to with our generosity.

- *Read the following proverbs. What do we learn about the*
  consequences of our attitude and actions toward the poor?

  14:21

  14:31

  17:5

  21:13

  22:9

- *Why do you suppose Yahweh is so concerned with our life's orientation toward the poor? What does this tell you about his own heart?*

❤ SHARE GOD'S HEART

Consider the biblical truth that all we own belongs to God, and we are merely managing whatever wealth he has entrusted to us. Jesus' parable on financial stewardship in Matthew 25, where the Master entrusted his servants with money, expecting them to invest it wisely, offers apt instruction in this regard. However much with which we've been entrusted, what we have is straight from the heart of God. He is the Master, we are the servants, and he longs for us to not only enjoy his own generosity but also to pass it forward. Matthew 25 implies "that money given in sacred offering to God will be returned with even more, by God's generosity."[51]

- *What might it look like in your own life to share from the storehouses of God's own generous heart toward you, letting generous giving to the poor "spring up freely from the joy of giving—all because God loves hilarious generosity" (2 Corinthians 9:7)?*

- *How do you think you might like to invest in those who are poor and oppressed? Take some time to consider such passion projects, then make a plan to share what has come to you from the generous heart of God.*

Greed Has No Bounds

The book of Proverbs begins with greed and ends with greed, chapters 1 and 30. In 1:10, we find a gang of sinful men enticing the son of the Teacher to join them in violently seizing what others have. "They'll resort to murder to steal their victim's assets," we find in Proverbs 1:18, "but eventually it will be their own lives that are ambushed."

While many of us would disavow the violence and ill-gotten gain the passage speaks about, "We read on," remarks scholar Paul Koptak, "perhaps even past the proverb, and miss its point about greed," which he defines in this way: "Greed can be defined as desire that knows no bounds, desire so strong that it does not care what is done to satisfy it or what harm it does to others."[52] Western believers are especially susceptible to this sinful condition, given that our economy and media are built on consumption.

- *What sorts of things do people desire, insatiably so? How have you seen this desire manifested in your own life?*

- *"A greedy man is in a race to get rich," Proverbs 28:22 reveals, "but he forgets that he could lose what's most important and end up with nothing." Connect this revelation-truth to the definition of greed.*

- *What does 28:22 reveal awaits the greedy? Why do you suppose this is the case?*

- *Proverbs 30:15 offers another definition of greed. How does it describe such people? In what way is greed connected to craving, and why is it never satisfied?*

Heavenly Treasure

Proverbs gives vast, deep wisdom for how we should think about issues of money, wealth, and generosity, as well as their converse: debt, poverty, and greed. Of course, we all know what Jesus said about the subject: "Don't keep hoarding for yourselves earthly treasures that can be stolen by thieves...Instead, stockpile heavenly treasures for yourselves that cannot be stolen and will never rust, decay, or lose their value. For your heart will always pursue what you value as your treasure" (Matthew 6:19–21). Where is your heart? What do you pursue? Is it generosity or greed? May these wise words cultivate in you a generous heart.

Talking It Out

1. What is your posture toward the resources with which the Lord has blessed you—whether time, treasures, or talents? On a scale of 1 to 10, rate both your generosity and greed, with 1 being the worst and 10 being the best, honestly assessing how you are walking in awe-filled worship of the Lord in these ways. Why did you rate yourself in these ways? Where is there room for growth?

2. As mentioned, Spurgeon exhorts, "Give then, and it shall be given unto you, good measure, pressed down, and running over." In your own life, how have you seen the truth of this exhortation, which echoes Jesus' own in Luke 6:38. When have you given and received a blessing in return?

3. When it comes to the poor specifically, how generous are you with the resources God has entrusted to you? How might you open up your heart toward those in need with the same generosity God himself opens up his heart?

4. Describe a life of generosity toward the poor—from government and society to churches and missions to individuals and families. How does your life match this picture of generosity—in your city, church, family, and your own life?

LESSON 9

Love vs. Hate

"What is love?" is a question that goes beyond a top-charting 1990s dance hit. It gets at the human condition, what we were made to do. After all, Jesus boiled down the entirety of the law to loving God and loving our neighbor. We also find love at the center of our most heated cultural debates; "love is love" is the new anthem, defining it in radical directions. According to these new definitions, love is rooted in how we feel—whether for our tribe or race, our own gender or the opposite. Far from being wise, it leads to foolishness all the way.

What is *biblical* love, then?

The common verb and noun for "love" are used in the book of Proverbs, "An inner quality expressed outwardly as a commitment to seek the well-being of the other through concrete acts of service," for both secular and sacred relationships.[53] However, there is another deeper word that expressed deeper love: *hesed*. Used nine times in Proverbs alone, this kind of love "is a type of loyalty that does not merely meet an obligation but goes the second mile...This linguistic compound representing one virtue piled atop another expresses a special and remarkable beneficence."[54]

Of course, the opposite of love is hate, but it is more than that. Anger, rage, and cruelty are antecedents that run contrary to the sort of selfless, outward commitment the Lord calls us into: a wise commitment rooted in our awe-filled worship of the One who has poured out his loyal love upon us in full measure.

Proverbs 3:3 exhorts, "Hold on to loyal love and don't let go." This is wise advice, which runs counter to our culture, which not only insists on being loyal to Number One, ourselves, but also centralizes the animating motivation for love entirely within ourselves, our feelings, and desires.

There is a different way, a wiser way that roots love in awe-filled worship of the One who loved us first. Let's explore how to be loyal lovers.

The Fear of the Lord Is the Beginning of Love

- *What do love and hate mean? Feel free to use a Bible dictionary or a website like www.biblestudytools.com but also give an initial definition from what you already understand.*

- *Now how do you suppose a proper attitude before God, living in obedient devotion to him with healthy fear, leads to a love-filled life? Why does awe-filled worship orient our heart around loyal love and mercy?*

- *Consider the opposite, when we refuse to worship Yahweh in awe and reverential fear. How does this choice lead to a hateful life? Why is refusing to fear God and worship him in awe the path of hate, anger, and rage?*

Cling to Loyal Love

There is a kind of love that runs deeper than mere affection, for both God and other people. It certainly transcends the ephemeral, self-interested sort of erotic love that evaporates at the end of a one-night stand. This love is rooted in God himself and our awe-filled worship of him, a posture of holy fear that responds to his radical love by turning it right back around toward others. Proverbs 3:3 urges us to "Hold on to loyal love and don't let go," tying and binding it around our neck and writing it on our heart. In other words, clinging so tightly to loyal love that our will and conscience are shaped by it.

- *How do you typically express love? Is it hard for you to give it or even receive it? Do you have pain or struggle associated with this word?*

ℶ WORD WEALTH

The Bible uses several words to express this deepest of human emotions and desires. The most common New Testament word for love is *agape*, the highest and deepest sense of the word. *Phileo* is another, used mostly to express intimate human affection and tender friendship, along with *eros* describing sexual intimacy and passionate love. The Hebrew is a bit different, where we find both kinds of love in this book.

Used over thirty times in Proverbs, the verb *'ahev* and corresponding noun *'ohev* for "love" are the most common forms in the Old Testament. Meaning "affection both pure and impure, divine and human,"[55] this love sits at the heart of Israel's central creed, the *Shemah*: "Love the Lord your God with every passion of your heart, with all the energy of your being, and with every thought that is within you."[56] Likewise, it is used in Leviticus 19:18, "You must love your friend in the same way you love yourself."[57]

There is a deeper Hebrew form of love, however, that transcends mere commitment and passion. *Hesed* is the word, and it is sometimes translated "loving-kindness" or "loyal love." You could also say it is one-way love, whether from God or people. "Behavior worthy of the term must be generous: a virtue unilaterally bestowed and usually associated with the party that holds the social advantage...This aspect of loving-kindness helps explain its popularity in descriptions of God: God's demonstrated loyalty to creation has an uncoerced, gracious quality."[58]

- *Compare and contrast the difference between the Hebrew nouns 'ohev and hesed. What is the difference between love and loyal love? How should hesed manifest itself in our day-to-day lives with others—whether our spouses, children, friends, or coworkers?*

- *Read the eight instances from the book of Proverbs where this special Hebrew word hesed occurs, sometimes translated as "kindness," "faithful love," and "tender mercies." What do you notice about how this kind of love should shape our relationships? Make a list of all that it means for the wise way of love.*

  11:17

  14:22

  16:6

  19:22

  20:6

20:28

21:21

31:26

 EXPERIENCE GOD'S HEART

God's heart is filled to the brim with *hesed*, with loyal love. John the Beloved sings the praises of this kind of love: "Look with wonder at the depth of the Father's marvelous love that he has lavished on us! He has called us and made us his very own beloved children" (1 John 3:1). Paul takes this realization comprehension further: "But Christ proved God's passionate love for us by dying in our place while we were still lost and ungodly!" (Romans 5:8) There is God's *hesed* heart on full display! The loyal love of God extended to us even when we rebelled against him, meeting us in a radical encounter that gathered us into his family. It is only when we fully grasp the depths of this love, the Father's loyalty to us despite our sinfulness, that we can fully love the world. After all, "Our love for others is our grateful response to the love God first demonstrated to us" (1 John 4:19).

- *Consider all the ways that God's marvelous loyal love has been lavished on you. How have you encountered the hesed heart of God? How has he been loyal to you despite your own faithlessness toward him? How should this marvelous encounter with God's hesed heart, in all of its ways, shape your own heart of love to others, clinging to the Lord's same loyal love in relationship with those you know?*

The Love of a Friend

With the advent of social media and the splintering of community, it's no surprise that most people haven't made any new friends in five years and have only two to five close friends. Despite all the promises of greater connectedness through online community, people feel lonelier than ever. And with Twitter followers and Facebook friends replacing actual relationships, we might wonder why we need flesh-and-blood friends to begin with. Proverbs explains why.

The themes of friendship and brotherhood (or sisterhood, as the case may be) are prominent in this book of wisdom. Perhaps this is because love is such an important thread running through Proverbs and you can't love unless you are in relationship. It's also because we were created for community. After all, when God created mankind, he said it was not good for them to be alone. Tied to friendship are broader themes of honesty, trust, companionship, and forgiveness.

- *Read through the following verses on friendship from Proverbs. What do you learn, and how does Proverbs teach you to love well as a friend?*

3:28

17:9

17:17

12:26

27:5–6

- *In light of these verses on friendship and love, how can you be a better friend this week to those who are part of your community?*

Simple Love Is Better

Love begins in the home. And sometimes the only thing a family has is love. Not a two-story home with four bedrooms but a ranch-style, three-bedroom home for a family of six. Not dinner out each week but home-cooked meals around a table set for two. Not trips to Disneyland each spring break but Saturday mornings to the local beach a few times in the summer.

The point here is the same one Proverbs makes: "It's much better to live simply, surrounded in holy awe and worship of God, than to have great wealth with a home full of trouble. It's much better to have a meal of vegetables surrounded with love and grace than a steak where there is hate" (15:16–17). The writer goes on in 17:1, bringing an exclamation point to the end of his exhortation: "A simple, humble life with peace and quiet is far better than an opulent lifestyle with nothing but quarrels and strife at home."

- *Are you pursuing a simple life of love, or is your heart captured by the high life? What affect do you think your pursuit of simple love has on your relationships—whether good or bad?*

- *How have you experienced the truth of these proverbs, where love is joined to simplicity? What has been the result?*

The Love of a Father

One of the hardest aspects of parenting is discipline. Not just the struggle sessions with a child to shape and mold them into the boy or girl—and eventually the man or woman—God has called them to be, but the heartrending act of denying them their time and treasures as a consequence for misbehavior. Parents want the best for their children, and sometimes that requires discipline.

The writer of Proverbs likens this loving, caring act to our heavenly Father's own love for us: "For the Father's discipline comes only from his passionate love and pleasure for you. Even when it seems like his correction is harsh, it's still better than any father on earth gives to his child" (3:12). Longman explains the parallel: "God corrects out of love. He does not want his people to continue in life-damaging attitudes and behaviors. The analogy that the father presents is that of a father who treats his son favorably. This is particularly poignant since the discourse is the loving admonition of a father to his son. Correction, though painful, is thus seen as a favor, a sign of grace."[59]

The writer of Proverbs offers further exhortations to parents: "Don't be afraid to discipline your children while they're still young enough to learn" (19:18); "Although rebellion is woven into a young man's heart, tough discipline can make him into a man" (22:15); "Don't withhold appropriate discipline from your child. Go ahead and punish him when he needs it. Don't worry—it won't kill him!" (23:13).

- *What are your thoughts on disciplining, and what has been your experience with it? Is it something you struggle with or have found value in? Explain.*

- *In a book on wisdom and wise living, why do you suppose discipline is a key, even loving component of wisdom training?*

- *If parents love their children, why is discipline one of the most loving acts? In what way does it reflect the heart of God himself?*

God Hates Hate

In previous lessons, we have explored how Proverbs 6:16–19 reveals God's true hatred for seven things, including pride, deceit, and wickedness. There are two more we can add to the list: "plotting evil in your heart toward another" and "stirring up strife between friends" (vv. 18, 19), each of which have hateful designs against others, not love.

Scholar Paul Koptak reveals this passage rephrases and intensifies the description of the scoundrel or "the wayward and wicked" man of verses 12–15, a reoccurring figure in Proverbs who "uses hatred as a weapon" to devise all sorts of wicked schemes.[60] Hate, then, is at the root of everything listed in this chapter.

- *Explain why human hatred lies at the root of this list of things God hates.*

- *What does this tell you about the heart of God that he hates hate, whether scheming wickedness toward another person from a heart of hate and anger or stirring up hateful strife between others?*

Hate's Fallout: Anger

Hate has consequences. Not merely eternal, given it is rooted in sin, and "Everyone who keeps hating a fellow believer is a murderer, and you know that no murderer has eternal life residing in him" (1 John 3:15), but also practical consequences, in the here and now with our relationships.

"Hatred keeps old quarrels alive," Proverbs 10:12 reveals, "but love draws a veil over every insult and finds a way to make sin disappear." The contrast here is striking. So is hatred's fallout, where wounds fester and the embers of old conflict continue inflaming relationships, leading to anger and resentment.

- *Read through the following proverbs. What do you learn about anger, its effects, and how we should respond to this fallout of a hate-filled heart?*

    12:28

    16:32

    19:19

    21:14

- *In what way does anger come from a heart that also struggles with hate? How might the two be linked?*

Love Conquers Hate

Instead of anger and hate, God invites us into a different kind of life, where walking in righteousness leads us to let go of such sinful emotions and instead share his heart of love with others. Consider Proverbs 10:12 again: "Hatred keeps old quarrels alive, but love draws a veil over every insult and finds a way to make sin disappear." In place of sinful anger is divinely drenched forgiveness; love truly trumps hate.

But it's more than that, more than merely trumping hate or getting over anger. There is an active posture to it, where the wrongs we've endured and the ones who have wronged us are overlooked and forgiven, where past failures no longer matter and hate is actively conquered by our love.

 SHARE GOD'S HEART

Consider Proverbs 17:9, "Love overlooks the mistakes of others, but dwelling on the failures of others devastates friendships," and 10:12, "Hatred keeps old quarrels alive, but love draws a veil over every insult and finds a way to make sin disappear."

- *What do you think about the wisdom of these two proverbs, 10:12 and 17:9? Does this sort of veil-drawing and mistake-overlooking come easily for you, or does it pose a challenge? Explain.*

- *Who in your life has wronged you, even hated you, bringing an anger-filled divide in your relationship? How might it look to heed the wisdom of these proverbs, conquering their hate by sharing the loving heart of God?*

Worship, Don't Hate

We end this lesson in the way we began it: with holy awe, with the fear of the Lord. There are times when we are wronged, when the evil of this world presses in against us and our family, threatening our work, our kids, our hearts. Although we may be tempted to lash out in anger, even coming to hate the one who is perpetrating evil against us, the book of Proverbs shows us a better way.

"Don't allow the actions of evil men," 23:17 exhorts, "to cause you to burn with anger. Instead, burn with unrelenting passion as you worship God in holy awe."

- *It seems like the writer of Proverbs is setting up fearing the Lord as an antidote to anger, even hate. What does worshiping God in holy awe do for us when we are at the brunt end of evil acts? Why do you suppose fearing the Lord offers exactly what we need in the face of wickedness?*

Love's Way

"Hold on to loyal love and don't let go" is wise advice. After all, "Our love for others is our grateful response to the love God first demonstrated to us" (1 John 4:19). That we love others because the Lord first loved us is basic Christian truth. It is equally true that our love begins with loving Yahweh, passionately responding to him with awe-filled worship for who he is and what he has done for us—empowering us to control our anger and instead share his heart of love. May we walk the wise way of love, the way Christ first paved before us.

Talking It Out

1. "Love overlooks the mistakes of others" (Proverbs 17:9).
   How are you at following these wise ways of love,
   overlooking and forgiving what others do, even to you?
   When was a time you followed through with this wisdom,
   and how did it turn out?

2. Do you struggle with anger? If so, where do you suppose
   this comes from, and what might you learn from this book
   of wisdom?

3. Friendship is a prominent theme in Proverbs because we were made for community. Proverbs 27:17 reminds us, "It takes a grinding wheel to sharpen a blade, and so one person sharpens the character of another." Who has sharpened you the most, offering their loving friendship to shape your life? How can you offer the same kind of sharpening this week?

4. When have you experienced a time when "the actions of evil men" caused you "to burn with anger" or at least threatened to cultivate hatred in your heart? What happened, what was that like, and how did you respond?

LESSON 10

Justice vs. Injustice

Rightness, justice, and fairness. Social justice and economic equity.

Whether fighting against misogyny, racism, or poverty, our culture has been searching for a way to right past and present wrongs—with decidedly unjust results. So where do we find the sort of rightness, justice, and fairness our world longs for? How do we achieve them for the sake of human flourishing and God's kingdom?

Proverbs 1:3 offers a clue: "Those who cling to these words will receive discipline to demonstrate wisdom in every relationship and to choose what is right and just and fair."

What is right and just and fair. Isn't this what our world is longing to establish—in corporations and neighborhoods, across racial and gender barriers—yet finding so hard to achieve in our institutions, in ourselves? Where is hope found for the sort of justice that is long-lasting and sturdy, the kind that leads to peace, reconciliation, and harmony? Social justice is what our world is demanding. The only problem is that true justice isn't social at all or rooted in our human gumption and ingenuity. Like all things that matter, true and lasting justice is rooted in God, his character, and his agenda.

In a *social* sense, "justice is understood as fairness, correct treatment, or equitable distribution of resources, but biblical justice is more than a mathematical distribution of goods." In a *biblical* sense, justice is "a chief attribute of God, with biblical justice inextricably tied to God's mercy and grounded in the relationship between God and humankind…Justice is rooted in God's character, and justice is what God demands of followers."[61]

Injustice is often measured by how the poor, marginalized, and oppressed are treated by the community, with strong calls for repentance against such affronts to God's own character, which makes sense. Because, as we have explored throughout this study, the way of wisdom, out of which the way of justice flows, is rooted in our submission to Yahweh—whether we approach him and his way with awe-filled worship. Only a proper fear of the Lord will ever lead to a properly ordered society, where justice reigns and human relationships are marked by fairness.

Justice isn't social; it's biblical. That doesn't lessen its importance; it elevates it to a standard even higher than that which our cultural warriors and government advocates champion. Those with ears to hear and eyes to see will pay close attention to what the book of Proverbs says. Read with care, listen closely, cling to these words: "Choose what is right and just and fair" (1:3).

The Fear of the Lord Is the Beginning of Justice

- *What do justice and injustice mean? Feel free to use a Bible dictionary or a website like www.biblestudytools. com but also give an initial definition from what you already understand.*

- *Now how do you suppose a proper mindset before God, living in obedient devotion to him with healthy fear, leads to a life of justice? Why does awe-filled worship orient our heart around rightness, justice, and fairness?*

- *Consider the opposite, when we refuse to worship Yahweh in awe and reverential fear. How does this mindset lead to an unjust life? Why is refusing to fear God and worship him in awe the path of injustice?*

God Hates Injustice

Throughout this study, we have explored several things the Lord Yahweh hates: lying and deception, pride, wickedness and hate, the wicked and their plans. Although *hate* may sound strong, the reality is that God hates sin, for it ruins his good creation and promotes the way things are not supposed to be. Injustice is something else God hates. Proverbs 17:15 offers an example of injustice on display and God's reaction: "There is nothing God hates more than condemning the one who is innocent and acquitting the one who is guilty."

Explaining this verse, Old Testament scholar Bruce Waltke reveals, "This proverb corrects the popular misconception that it is better to set free ten guilty persons than to condemn one innocent person. Both are an abomination to the Lord."[62] The reason why is that both are unjust, whether denying the innocent justice or refusing to dole out just punishment to the guilty. God hates them equally because God hates injustice.

- *The Hebrew word here for "hate" can also mean "abominate" or "detest," showing the severity of God's response. Why do you suppose injustice elicits such a strong response from the Lord? How should his response inform our own?*

God Fights for Justice

It isn't only that God hates injustice. He also loves justice and actively fights for it. He is the champion of those oppressed by those in power, pleading their case and caretaking those used and abused by self-interested individuals and social systems of power. Consider two examples: the widow and the poor.

"The Lord champions the widow's cause," Proverbs 15:25 explains, "but watch him as he smashes down the houses of the haughty!" We saw this in lesson 7, but it is worth noting again. Proverbs 22:22–23 further describes the depths to which Yahweh will go in his fight to make things right in the world: "Never oppress the poor or pass laws with the motive of crushing the weak. For the Lord will rise to plead their case and humiliate the one who humiliates the poor."

- *What does it reveal about the heart of God that he "champions" the oppressed cause and "pleads their case"? What is it about widows and the poor that seems to draw the Lord's attention so consistently? What should this tell us about what he cares about and what our concerns should be as well?*

♥ EXPERIENCE GOD'S HEART

Oftentimes, issues of justice and injustice aren't abstract; they're personal. Whether we're part of a racial group that has been discriminated against, a member of a lower economic class, or even a widow who is neglected and overlooked—God's heart for justice means something for us!

- *What does it mean to you personally that Yahweh champions and pleads the cause and case of the oppressed? How would you like to experience the heart of God in this way—when it comes to racial, economic, or religious justice?*

The Righteous Respond to Injustice

As followers of Jesus Christ, we are called to love the things God loves, to hate the things God hates. As we saw in the previous question, God loves fighting for the just cause of those trampled by injustice. Proverbs calls us into this same attitude: "The wicked hate those who live a godly life, but the righteous hate injustice wherever it's found" (29:27). Of course, hate is only half the story; we are called to love justice as much as to hate injustice. As Proverbs 16:8 exhorts, "It is better to have little with a heart that loves justice than to be rich and not have God on your side."

- *Consider your relationship with the words justice and injustice. Do you approach them with the same emotion as the Lord does, with hate and love? Explain.*

- *"When you take a secret bribe," Proverbs 17:23 says, "your actions reveal your true character, for you pervert the ways of justice." This is one example of ways we may "pervert the ways of justice," unwittingly or not. Take time to reflect on ways you may undermine God's cause to make things right, fair, and equal in the world. Then ask the Holy Spirit to use these wise words of Proverbs to right your heart around God's own.*

In contrast to the posture of the righteous toward justice and injustice, the ungodly have a very different response: "God's righteous people will pour themselves out for the poor, but the ungodly make no attempt to understand or help the needy" (29:7).

- *Compare and contrast how the righteous and ungodly respond to this example of injustice, poverty. In what do you suppose their mutual responses are rooted? What's at the heart of their response?*

- *How might you be part of the solution by pouring yourself out for the poor?*

❤ SHARE GOD'S HEART

It is clear from Proverbs and the entire counsel of Scripture that the Lord desires his righteous ones to actively join him in pleading the case of the poor and oppressed, becoming their champions for justice!

- *Do you have a burning desire to champion the oppressed and plead their case for justice, to share this aspect of the heart of God as revealed in Proverbs 15:25 and 22:22–23? Explain.*

- *If not, spend time asking the Lord to cultivate within you a desire to share his heart of justice. If there is something specific, offer a tangible way you can make progress this week in sharing this aspect of God's heart.*

The Pleadings of the Poor

The revelation-truth unveiled in Proverbs 18:23 is as true today as it was back then: "The poor plead for help from the rich, but all they get in return is a harsh response." One of the more modern manifestations of this so-called "help" is the payday loan. These short-term, high-cost loans for amounts usually less than $500 seem specifically targeted at the impoverished—you never find these outfits in upper-class neighborhoods. With interest rates ranging from 391 percent to more than 521 percent, this seems like a case-in-point of the harsh response condemned by the proverb. Proverbs 28:8 condemns this sort of practice: "Go ahead and get rich on the backs of the poor, but all the wealth you gather will one day be given to those who are kind to the needy."

Longman offers apt commentary on this indictment against the rich here, not only celebrating wealth as a sign of wisdom and God's blessing but also condemning illegitimate ways wealth is accumulated through charging interest rates, especially obscene amounts as illustrated above. He writes, "Charging interest to fellow Israelites was against the law. Here the consequence is that wealth would be taken away and given to someone who would be kind to the poor...the implicit assumption may be that these people are gouging the poor by charging them interest but that whatever material is gained by the strategy will be returned to the poor."[63] Here we find a reversal, where the riches of the wealthy are handed over to the poor in some way.

- *One example was offered above, where the wealthy exploit the poor's pleadings with a harsh response through payday loans. What is another example that might be similarly harsh?*

- *What does it mean to you to know that someday, somehow, God will ensure that inappropriately gained wealth is returned to the poor? What does this promise say about God and his heart for the poor?*

 THE EXTRA MILE

The prophet Amos offers a scathing indictment against Israelites who wallowed in their wealth and did nothing for the poor. As New Testament scholar Craig Blomberg explains, "Speaking to the wealthy Israelite women and then to their male counterparts, Amos unleashes a tirade on how they wallow in their luxuries while caring not a whit for the acute suffering of their countrymen, including those whom they have themselves exploited."[64]

He goes on to offer several contemporary equivalents: "the highest amounts of money spent on entertainment, food, and drink (including alcohol), and fancy rooms in luxury hotels for business and academic gatherings, vacations on extravagant cruise liners or at costly theme parks, or even the 'routine expenses' of regularly eating (and drinking) out in fancy restaurants, precisely while people whom we could have helped are dying of preventable illness all around the world."[65]

- *Read Amos 6:1–7. The prophet reflects these same proverbs, underscoring wealthy indulgence at the expense of the poor. The prophet speaks "woes" against those who live in luxurious comfort. What does Amos say will be the punishment for such people? Along with these proverbs, why should this prophetic passage serve as a warning for all who live in economic comfort?*

Leaders and the Fight for the Poor

The book of Proverbs often specifically addresses those in power, offering special exhortations for leaders and rulers. The powerful are commanded to fight for justice in three ways: "Be a righteous king, judging on behalf of the poor and interceding for those most in need" (31:9). Be…judge…intercede—on behalf of the poor and those in need.

- *People in power are uniquely positioned to both help and hinder the poor and marginalized in society. What does it tell you about the heart of God that he would offer these three imperatives to fight for economic justice?*

- *Give an example of what it might look like in the world for those in power to actively intercede on behalf of the poor? How might it look in your own life to heed this wisdom?*

God's Pleasure in Justice

We have already explored God's heart for the poor and oppressed and how the righteous are called to respond to injustice around us. Proverbs 21:3 takes this exploration a step further, revealing how much pleasure God takes when we actively seek to model and establish justice in the world: "It pleases God more when we demonstrate godliness and justice than when we merely offer him a sacrifice."

This is quite the revelation! For sacrifices were no small part of Israel's national and spiritual life. The Lord instituted specific laws for offering him grain or animals on specific occasions to atone for their sins. We find many of these laws in the earliest part of Leviticus, chapters 1–6. These sacrifices were not an insignificant part of their worship; they were legally required. To be sure, the Lord loved their sacrifices. What we find here, however, is that he loves our demonstrations of justice *more than* all the sacrifices we could offer!

- *While we don't offer the grain, bird, and lamb sacrifices of Israel, what sorts of sacrifices do we offer to the Lord in our own spiritual lives as believers? Why do you suppose the Lord cares more about justice than these offerings?*

- *Longman notes, "It might be argued from the proverb and elsewhere that sacrifice without righteousness and justice is worthless."[66] Explain.*

The Joy of Justice

In recent years, there have been a rash of cases involving death-row inmates who were waiting to receive their punishment only for authorities to discover that the person serving the crime didn't match newly uncovered DNA evidence. If you were one of those wrongly accused people, or a family member or friend, the only proper response would be singing, shouting, and dancing.

For not only was an unjust verdict overturned with the light of truth, but a life was also spared and the right person convicted. Proverbs 21:15 speaks to this impulse for finding joy in justice: "When justice is served, the lovers of God celebrate and rejoice, but the wicked begin to panic."

• *Have you had cause to "celebrate and rejoice" after justice was served? If so, what happened, and what was that like to have justice served on your own behalf?*

• *Why is justice a cause for celebration and rejoicing wherever we find it?*

The Source of Justice

At the heart of justice is a profound sense of equality and rightness, that things are exactly the way they are supposed to be in the world before sin ruined it all. Whether between ethnicities or classes, in households and companies. We know the source of injustice is the wickedness of the human heart, for from it flows the inequality, unfairness, and wickedness aimed squarely at the poor, oppressed, and marginalized.

What about the source of *justice*? Is it found in Congress or the president, in corporations and civic groups, in social justice warriors and celebrities? Proverbs 29:26 reminds us of the true source: "Everyone curries favor with leaders. But God is the judge, and justice comes from him."

- *How should this verse guide our understanding of what justice is and how it should look in the world? What is the difference between justice from God and justice from government (or culture or corporations or celebrities)? Explain.*

The Just Cause

Proverbs offers a wealth of wisdom to heal our divisions, put to right the injustices of our day, and to set a course that truly unveils the fullness of God's kingdom-life here on earth as it is in heaven. Not only does Proverbs offer encouragement for the oppressed, but it also exhorts those in power to carefully consider how their actions affect other people and society, along with special warnings. May we adopt Proverbs' same passion for justice and perspective on injustice, making the cause of the poor and oppressed our own cause—all for the sake of Christ and his kingdom.

Talking It Out

1. Give an example of a modern injustice God hates. How should God's response inform our own, and what might you and your community be able to do about it?

2. When we find more fervent responses to the poor and other social injustices coming from ungodly sources, like the government or corporations, than from the church, what does that say about the righteous? Do you think God's righteous lovers, the church, generally have a good reputation in this area, or is there room for improvement? Explain.

3. Consider from the earlier question the list of "sacrifices" we believers often offer the Lord—whether sacrifices of praise and prayer, tithing and special gifts, our time and talents. When it comes to prioritizing these sacrifices and issues of justice, how do these areas match up? Do you focus more on sacrifices than on justice or the other way around? Explain.

LESSON 11

Order vs. Disorder

In the mid-1990s, a curious set of self-help books instantly rocketed to bestseller status: *Chicken Soup for the Soul.* The publishers named it as such "because they wanted it to soothe and provide comfort, just like their grandmothers' cooking."[67] Since then, it has turned into a self-help juggernaut of more than 275 books, an entertainment streaming division, and actual cans of soup and other prepared foods. A practical guide to the good life is what these books sell, and over 110 million people are buying it.

In the introductory lesson, we noted how much of the wise words found in the book of Proverbs are not merely theological musings without practical insight. Although thoroughly rooted in Yahweh and a response of worshipful awe, anyone seeking practical advice for human flourishing and a fulfilling life will find what they are longing for in this book. One of those areas of practical advice shared by contemporary self-help books like *Chicken Soup for the Soul* is creating a disciplined, planned, productive life that delivers the good life.

You may not think about Proverbs in this light, but order and disorder are broad categories for much of the wisdom words in this book. Guarding your words and sex life in self-control is high on Proverbs' list of a well-ordered life oriented around fearing Yahweh. Those who don't control their "self" allow it to carry them "away as hostages—kidnapped captives robbed of destiny" (5:23).

Instead, we are to be disciplined. Not only in the sense of

living a disciplined life, for "Although rebellion is woven into a young man's heart, tough discipline can make him into a man" (22:15). But also leaning into being disciplined and disciplining others. This wisdom has bearing on parents as they seek to shape their children into well-ordered lovers of God, as well as on us as we receive the Lord's correction as a loving Father.

A disordered person, however, shuns discipline, never learning from mistakes and refusing to be trained by them. He or she is out of control, letting body parts run wild and living a lazy life, never planning or preparing for the future. Although preparing for the future requires trusting our plans to the Lord with care and seeking advice for how we strategize for the future, well-ordered people activate their imaginations for their preferred life rather than letting that life simply happen to them.

Discover how to order your life in such a way that it is marked by wisdom from above!

The Fear of the Lord Is the Beginning of Order

- *What do order and disorder mean when it comes to a life controlled by wisdom, from self-control to planned work? Feel free to use a Bible dictionary or a website like www. biblestudytools.com but also give an initial definition from what you already understand.*

- *Now how do you suppose a proper response before God, living in obedient devotion to him with healthy fear, leads to a well-ordered life? Why does awe-filled worship orient our heart around a life of order and self-control?*

- *Consider the opposite, when we refuse to worship Yahweh in awe and reverential fear. How does this response lead to a disordered, undisciplined life? Why is refusing to fear God and worship him in awe the path of disorder?*

Godly Instruction for a Well-Ordered Life

How do we live a well-ordered life? One that not only conforms to the ordered way of life God intended things to be when he created the world but one that also brings enjoyment and is productive not for enjoyment and productivity purely for their own sake but for the glory of the Lord and good of others? Godly instruction leads to such a life.

In Proverbs 6:20–23 a father exhorts his son to obey "godly instruction and follow your mother's life-giving teaching," to fill his heart with her advice and let his life be shaped by her counsel.

- *In a basic sense, how might godly instructions guide one's life choices, leading to a good life—even a well-ordered one?*

- *What sort of godly instruction have you received from your own parents? How has it filled your heart and shaped your life, offering guidance and wisdom to order your life?*

The writer goes on: "Their wisdom will guide you wherever you go and keep you from bringing harm to yourself. Their instruction will whisper to you at every sunrise and direct you through a brand-new day. For truth is a bright beam of light shining into every area of your life, instructing and correcting you to discover the ways to godly living."

Guidance, direction, instruction, and correction—leading to godly living. What the father shares with his son is wisdom and discernment steeped in awe-filled worship and fear of the Lord—and that's why it leads to godly living.

- *Godly living is well-ordered living, for it reflects the heart of God for us. Where do you typically find guidance, direction, instruction, and correction to know how to live an ordered life oriented around the heart of God? How does this compare with God's wisdom?*

 EXPERIENCE GOD'S HEART

As we've seen, godly living is well-ordered living, for it reflects the heart of God for us.

- *Where does our culture typically find guidance, direction, instruction, and correction to know how to live an ordered life? How about you, especially when it comes to orienting and ordering your life around the heart of God?*

- *How do you think these sources for wisdom compare to God's wisdom? In what way might encountering his heart of guidance, direction, instruction, and correction shape your life in ways that will put it into godly order? Explain.*

Plan in Step with the Lord

Westerners are planners. An entire industry exists to help us wring as much productivity from our day as possible, ordering our lives, and making something of it. While making plans and planning our day, even an entire year, with care is a good thing, there is a danger in relying purely on our own gumption and ingenuity to order our lives, as well-intentioned as we are to reflect God's own well-ordered, deliberate heart.

As with everything in life, Proverbs brings us back to the basics, even when it comes to planning our lives. Consider 16:1, 3, and 9: "Go ahead and make all the plans you want, but it's the Lord who will ultimately direct your steps...Before you do anything, put your trust totally in God and not in yourself. Then every plan you make will succeed...Within your heart you can make plans for your future, but the Lord chooses the steps you take to get there."

- *Ultimately, our steps are directed and our life is planned by the Lord. How reliant upon the Lord are you making your plans? Is he top of mind, where you go to him straight away in prayer? Or is he an afterthought, where you hand him your ready-made plans and ask for his blessing?*

- *Why do you suppose "[putting] your trust totally in God and not in yourself" before you do anything is the way to go? What does he offer our well-ordered planning that we cannot offer ourselves?*

DIGGING DEEPER

What role does free will play in our ordered planning? Is it all God and we're just along for the ride? Is it all us and God's just playing a bit part on our world stage? Consider what C. S. Lewis says about this dynamic between free will and God's will:

God created things which had free will.
That means creatures which can go either
wrong or right. Some people think they
can imagine a creature which was free
but had no possibility of going wrong; I
cannot. If a thing is free to be good it is
also free to be bad. And free will is what
has made evil possible. Why, then, did
God give them free will? Because free will,
though it makes evil possible, is also the
only thing that makes possible any love or
goodness or joy worth having. A world of
automata—of creatures that worked like
machines—would hardly be worth creating.
The happiness which God designs for His
higher creatures is the happiness of being
freely, voluntarily united to Him and to
each other in an ecstasy of love and delight
compared with which the most rapturous
love between a man and a woman on this
earth is mere milk and water. And for that
they must be free.[68]

- *Implicit in Lewis's commentary is the recognition that our
  will should be oriented around God's will—"voluntarily
  united to Him and to each other in an ecstasy of love and
  delight." So how do we know God's will, where do we
  discover it? How does Proverbs help us understand this
  will, the one that should inform our plans?*

Passionate Productivity

We create because God is a Creator; we are makers because we serve the Maker. It's no surprise that after he created us, he told us to not only enjoy his good creation and rule over it (Genesis 1:26–27) but to also make something out of it, working the land to shape it into orchards and skyscrapers, iPhones and glass bottles, Teslas and spaceships (2:15).

The apostle Paul reminds us, "Whether you eat or drink, live your life in a way that glorifies and honors God" (1 Corinthians 10:31). Proverbs offers similar reminders, exhorting us to passionate productivity: "A passive person won't even complete a project, but a passionate person makes good use of his time, wealth, and energy" (Proverbs 12:27).

- *In a book dedicated to wisdom and the wise life, why do you suppose passionate productivity is included?*

- *How are you putting to use your own time, wealth, and energy in passionate pursuit of making things out of God's world?*

- *Part of what it means to live a wise, well-ordered life is directing our passionate productivity in ways that provide for our livelihoods—food for our family and a roof over our heads. Read Proverbs 12:11, 14:23, and 20:13. What do you learn about working for what we need?*

The Disorder of Self-Control

It might not be obvious at first, but people who lack self-control are people whose lives are disordered. They are held captive to their desires, rather than captivated by the heart of God. They are carried away by the members of their body, leading to chaos and disorder—not only in their own life but also in other people's lives, especially in their relationships.

Read the following proverbs. What do you learn about the disordered life that comes from failing to live a life of self-control?

5:23

7:25

13:3

14:17

25:16, 28

 SHARE GOD'S HEART

We know from Scripture that issues of self-control aren't simply about following lists of dos and don'ts. Instead, these wise words from Proverbs are meant to guide us into the kind of blessed life God intends for us, flowing not from a kill-joy heart but from his heart of radical love. Sometimes we need to be reminded of that, especially those of us whose lives are disordered.

- *What are areas of self-control in which you struggle—whether with food or drink, sex or relationships? How might these wise words from Proverbs not only guide you into the wise, blessed life the Lord intends for you but also enable a radical encounter with his heart of love?*

Don't Be a Sluggard

There is a remarkable word that is used only in the book of Proverbs. Often it is translated "lazy," contrasted with those who are diligent, like lowly ants that work hard and with great industry. The word is *sluggard*, the adjective *'atzel* that means "to be sluggish, lazy." It isn't just that they sleep in and let the dishes pile in the sink. It's that they sit around in their parent's basement and play video games all day or go to work and do their job half-heartedly or binge-watch TV instead of spending time with their children or even stay so busy with minor things that they don't have time to pray.

- *Read Proverbs 6:6–11. Why do you suppose the writer illustrates his wise exhortation with an ant in contrast to the sluggard? What is wisely ordered about the ant's way? What is foolishly disordered about the sluggard?*

 DIGGING DEEPER

Consider another passage, Proverbs 24:30–34:

> One day I passed by the field of a lazy man, and I noticed the vineyards of a slacker. I observed nothing but thorns, weeds, and broken-down walls. So I considered their lack of wisdom, and I pondered the lessons I could learn from this: Professional work habits prevent

poverty from becoming your permanent business partner. And: If you put off until tomorrow the work you could do today, tomorrow never seems to come.

English preacher Charles Spurgeon offers wise commentary that reveals the significance of the sluggard's life:

> The worst of sluggards only ask for a little slumber; they would be indignant if they were accused of thorough idleness. A little folding of the hands to sleep is all they crave, and they have a crowd of reasons to show that this indulgence is a very proper one. Yet by these littles the day ebbs out, and the time for labour is all gone, and the field is grown over with thorns. It is by little procrastinations that men ruin their souls... Like sands from an hour-glass, time passes, life is wasted by driblets, and seasons of grace lost by little slumbers.
>
> Oh, to be wise, to catch the flying hour, to use the moments on the wing! May the Lord teach us this sacred wisdom, for otherwise a poverty of the worst sort awaits us, eternal poverty which shall want even a drop of water, and beg for it in vain...O that men were wise be-times, and would seek diligently unto the Lord Jesus, or ere the solemn day shall dawn when it will be too late to plough and to sow, too late to repent and believe. In harvest, it is vain to lament that the seed time was neglected. As yet, faith and holy decision are timely. May we obtain them this night.[69]

- *In light of Spurgeon's commentary on this passage,*
  explain the gravity and seriousness of the sluggard's life.
  Why is it so serious, so foolish?

Four Disordered Parts of Society

First Corinthians 14:33 reminds us that God is a God of order and harmony, not disorder and confusion. And yet, there is much that is disordered in our world; people live confused lives. That's because of the fall, the moment when Mama Eve and Papa Adam rebelled against God, plunging his very good, ordered, and harmonious world into chaos, disorder, and death. Proverbs 30:21–23 clues us into this reality by outlining four disordered events that are intolerable to the Lord:

> There are four intolerable events
>   that are simply unbearable to observe:
> when an unfaithful servant becomes a
> ruler,
>   when a scoundrel comes into great
> wealth,
> when an unfaithful woman marries a good
> man,
>   and when a mistress replaces a faithful
> wife.

Old Testament scholar Paul Koptak explains the historical nuances behind these wise words: "Just as the 'way of an adulteress' (30:20) is out of step with the created order of wisdom, so the four items listed threaten to overturn that order. In ancient Near Eastern thinking, the earth shakes when the natural order is disturbed. The 'trembling' (30:21) of the earth is like the raging of the fool that disturbs peace in every sense of the word (cf. 29:9)."[70]

> These four events each depict a promotion undeserved, a displacing of one who is virtuous with one who is corrupt. Each promotion indicates that they will carry their corruption with them. The unfaithful servant will likely become a tyrant. The fool who becomes wealthy will squander his wealth. The unfaithful woman (or "hated woman") will continue her immorality even after she's married. The girlfriend who replaced the faithful wife will likely find another man one day.[71]

- *Why do you suppose these four events are so "intolerable" that they are out of order and might create social chaos?*

- *"To the sages, the social world had a definite order and hierarchy; when this order is disturbed, the 'earth trembles.'"[72] Where else have you seen in our own society the chaos that comes from disordered life? What has been the fallout?*

The Ordered Life

Like many self-help books, *Chicken Soup for the Soul* seeks to inspire people toward living the good life. These books share "happiness, inspiration, and hope," offering it through stories and anecdotes illustrating the sort of life readers can help themselves to. Although heeding the wisdom found in the book of Proverbs doesn't guarantee the good life, it sure points you on the pathway toward finding it. This life begins with a posture of holy awe, rooted in wisdom, and carried out with order—where self-control, discipline, and planning mark your life lived for God's glory and the world's good.

Talking It Out

1. What can we learn from humble ants in Proverbs 6 when it comes to our own hard work? In what areas of your life do you need to work hard and pray against disordered laziness?

2. Consider 27:1. When have you experienced what this verse warns against—bragging about the plans you have made or the order you brought to your day, week, month, and year— and then it fell apart? What happened, and is there a lesson to learn there?

3. Proverbs 19:21 reminds us, "A person may have many ideas concerning God's plan for his life, but only the designs of his purpose will succeed in the end." What "designs of his purpose" do you believe God has for your own life? What about for our lives spent together, such as in a family, with friends, or in a church?

4. Proverbs 30:22–23 depicts four areas of disorder that can lead to social chaos. How have you experienced the chaos that can come from disordered living, whether from these four illustrations or elsewhere? What was that like? What has happened?

LESSON 12

Purity vs. Pleasure

Throughout the Bible's Wisdom Literature, life is often presented as a fork in the road. From Psalms to Proverbs, Ecclesiastes to Song of Songs, there are two paths—one leading to life, the other to death. Like the Robert Frost poem, where "Two roads diverged in a yellow wood," we are invited to "[take] the one less traveled by," the one that makes all the difference.[73]

This study has been a lesson in diverging roads: truth in contrast to deceit, pride versus humility, the way of love instead of the way of hate, justice's road set against the way of injustice. Perhaps no other traveling road is as stark in our day and age than the way of pleasure versus purity, where our instant culture offers instant pleasure at the push of a button—summoning gossip and pornography on our devices, next-day delivery of vices, and a roadmap for diving into the depths of the "my-way" that leads to death.

And yet, there is another way. A way of purity and virtue in service of others that is decidedly set against the me-centered way. The most beautiful contrast to this self-centered life of pleasure is the so-called Proverbs 31 woman. She is a radiant bride, full of "strength and mighty valor!" (31:10). She is the model of purity, for she "brings [her husband] what is good and not evil" (v. 12), "searches out continually to possess that which is pure and righteous" (v. 13), and "watches over the ways of her household and meets every need they have" (v. 27).

What sets her apart is not only her pursuit of goodness and righteousness, the purity of her life, but also the purity of her purpose—which is decidedly other-centric. She "arises and sets food on the table for hungry ones in her house and for others" (v. 15), "stretches out her hands to help the needy" (v. 19), and "watches over the ways of her household and meets every need they have" (v. 27). All she does is good and glorious, from her handmade crafts to the management of house, from truthful teachings to wise ways.

Ultimately, "this virtuous woman lives in the wonder, awe, and fear of the Lord" (v. 30), the source of her purity and virtue. It isn't her charm or beauty; it isn't even her righteous works and loving acts of service. Instead, a worshipful awe of Yahweh centers her life, which anchors all the rest in the purity of his ways.

Pleasure is fleeting; purity is forever. Use this lesson to explore your current relationship with purity and pleasure, then prepare to take action under the fear of the Lord.

The Fear of the Lord Is the Beginning of Purity

- *What do purity and pleasure mean? Feel free to use a Bible dictionary or a website like www.biblestudytools. com but also give an initial definition from what you already understand.*

- *Now how do you suppose a proper posture before God, living in obedient devotion to him with healthy fear, leads to a virtuous life of purity? Why does awe-filled worship orient our heart around purity and virtue?*

- *Consider the opposite, when we refuse to worship Yahweh in awe and reverential fear. How does this posture lead to a life of fleeting pleasure? Why is refusing to fear God and worship him in awe the path of worldly pleasure?*

The Lord Loves Purity

Every lesson leading to this final one has been one of contrasts between what reflects the heart of God and what doesn't. Truth in contrast to lies and deceit. A generous heart instead of a greedy, selfish heart. Love versus hate. Among others, truth, generosity, and love all reflect the heart of God; they are the way he intends us to live. The same is true of living a pure life in contrast to a pleasure-filled one.

Consider Proverbs 15:9, "The Lord detests the lifestyle of the wicked, but he loves those who pursue purity." Proverbs 22:11 reflects the same attitude: "The Lord loves those whose hearts are holy, and he is the friend of those whose ways are pure." The Hebrew word here for purity is *tahor,* which can also be translated as "clean"—both ceremonially in our worship and ethically in our actions.

- *What do you suppose is meant by pure ways? Proverb 20:11 makes a contrast between character that is "pure or perverse." To better understand what is meant by pure ways, make a chart presenting additional contrasts between pure ways versus pleasure-filled ones.*

- *What is it about purity, in worship and actions, that the Lord loves so much? Why do you suppose it is important to him that we are pure in our ways?*

- *The early church theologian Athanasius remarked, "Even when the sinner looks for gratification, he doesn't find the fruit of his sin pleasant." Why not? Why does our pursuit of sinful pleasure ultimately not satisfy?*

Youthful Lusts: A Warning

Proverbs offers wisdom for every age and stage of life, for all occasions. However, one area the book of wisdom spends a great deal of time addressing is what could be called youthful lust. Promiscuity and the seduction of sexual sin can haunt men and women alike, whether young or middle-aged, married, or single. Yet the book has a special word straight from the heart of God for young men—concentrated in two full chapters: Proverbs 5 and 7.

Matthew Henry offers sound commentary on this instructive wisdom into pleasure and impurity, with insights on Proverbs 7:

> Here is an affecting example of the danger
> of youthful lusts. It is a history or a parable
> of the most instructive kind. Will any one
> dare to venture on temptations that lead
> to impurity, after Solomon has set before
> his eyes in so lively and plain a manner,
> the danger of even going near them? Then
> is he as the man who would dance on the
> edge of a lofty rock, when he has just seen
> another fall headlong from the same place.
> The misery of self-ruined sinners began in
> disregard to God's blessed commands. We

ought daily to pray that we may be kept
from running into temptation, else we invite
the enemies of our souls to spread snares
for us. Ever avoid the neighbourhood
of vice. Beware of sins which are said
to be pleasant sins. They are the more
dangerous, because they most easily gain
the heart, and close it against repentance.
Do nothing till thou hast well considered
the end of it. Were a man to live as long as
Methuselah, and to spend all his days in
the highest delights sin can offer, one hour
of the anguish and tribulation that must
follow, would far outweigh them.[74]

Youthful lusts offer everyone a warning, especially young men,
as the father writing to his son cautions. So, too, does Matthew
Henry: "Beware of sins which are said to be pleasant sins."

- *Read Proverbs 5:1–23 and 7:1–27. According to the
  writer, what dangers do sexual pleasures present,
  especially to young men?*

- *Proverbs 6:24–35 takes the discussion in a deeper
  direction: adultery. What does this passage say will
  protect people from this sort of immorality? Why do you
  suppose it is the antidote?*

EXPERIENCE GOD'S HEART

The issue of sexual sin, whether fornication or adultery, is one that is especially troublesome. Not only for young men but people from all ages and stages of life. Perhaps that's why the book of Proverbs spends so much time addressing it and why there are so many examples from Scripture of this sin at work leading people into unwise, wicked ways.

- *Have you struggled in this area? Have you stumbled into this sort of unwise, sinful way? If so, the hope of the heart of God is that his forgiveness, redemption, and new life is waiting for you with open arms! Seek that heart now, asking the Lord to open it up to you to experience all the wisdom he has for you when it comes to sexual purity—praying not only for forgiveness if you need it but also for supernatural strength to walk his wise way.*

The Foolishness of Drunkenness

The issue of alcohol is one that has vexed the church for centuries. Some have fought for prohibition, rightly identifying how other social ills are rooted in the abuse of alcohol. Others have pushed back against any limits on drinking, insisting Christian liberty allows for freely imbibing within reason. Still more have had individual experiences with it, whether struggling with alcoholism personally or experiencing the fallout in their families from alcohol abuse. At minimum, the book of Proverbs offers sound wisdom for handling alcohol while also addressing the sin of drunkenness.

- *What are your views on alcohol and drinking, and what might those views be rooted in, whether personal experience and baggage or the Bible?*

- *Read Proverbs 23:29–35 and 31:4–7. What do you learn about the pains and problems associated with drunkenness? How does the wisdom of living in awe-filled worship and fear of the Lord counteract alcohol abuse?*

♥ SHARE GOD'S HEART

The wisdom flowing out of the heart of God from the book of Proverbs isn't meant to kill our joy or keep us from enjoying life. Just the opposite! It saves us from heartache and helps us avoid foolish pitfalls—like the kind that comes from drunkenness. The Lord longs to unveil his heart for people, showing them the way of purity and truth that leads to the kind of life he has for those who seek his face.

- *Whom do you know who needs the wisdom of Proverbs that addresses drunkenness and drinking? How might it look to share with them these revelation-insights into the heart of God?*

- *Or are these wise words about alcohol just as applicable or perhaps more so to you than to others you know? If so, what can you do to follow their counsel?*

A Prayer for Purity

"Death and destruction are never filled," Proverbs 27:20 reveals, "and the desires of men's hearts are insatiable." We seek pleasure at every turn, never satisfied, always wanting more, which is why we need to plead with the heart of God to flood our heart with the satisfaction that only he can bring!

Proverbs 30:7–9 offers those who seek the heart of God a template for prayer, seeking after the things of his heart and denying themselves what is contrary:

God, there are two things I'm asking you
for before I die, only two:
Empty out of my heart everything that is
false—
every lie, and every crooked thing.
And give me neither undue poverty nor
undue wealth—
but rather, feed my soul with the
measure of prosperity
that pleases you.
May my satisfaction be found in you.
Don't let me be so rich that I don't need
you
or so poor that I have to resort to
dishonesty
just to make ends meet.
Then my life will never detract from
bringing glory to your name.

Lesson 5 also offered this as a prayer for lovers of God who long to be truth-tellers. It is offered again here with the specific intent to pray against the pleasures that seek to fill our heart— whether material or sexual, food or substances—and instead ask the Holy Spirit to fill us with the purity of Christ.

- *Take a moment to pray this prayer now, asking the Lord to empty your heart of every crooked desire, draining it of the world's pleasures in order to feed your soul with what is pure.*

The Hallmark of Purity

We end this lesson with perhaps the sharpest, high-definition picture of purity we could set our minds upon, illustrating not only a life saturated in purity but also a life walking in wisdom: the Radiant Bride, the Virtuous Woman. She is both a picture of a virtuous wife and an incredible allegory of the end-time victorious bride of Jesus Christ, full of virtue and grace. Consider how Gregory of Nazianzus, the fourth-century Archbishop of Constantinople, explained the majesty of this woman and her pure virtue:

> The divinely inspired Solomon in his
> instructive wisdom, I mean in his Proverbs,
> praises the woman who keeps her house
> and loves her husband. And in contrast
> to the woman who wanders abroad, who
> is uncontrolled and dishonorable, who
> hunts precious souls with wanton ways
> and words, he praises her who is engaged
> honorably at home, who performs her
> womanly duties with fearless courage,
> her hands constantly holding the spindle
> as she prepares double cloaks for her
> husband, who buys a field in season, and
> carefully provides food for her servants,
> and receives her friends at a bountiful
> table, and who exhibits all other qualities
> for which he extols in song the modest and
> industrious woman.[75]

Nazianzus wrote this commentary in praise of his own sister, whom he likened to the Proverbs 31 woman. It is a heroic hymn meant for all women who live "in the wonder, awe, and fear of the Lord" (v. 30)!

- *Read Proverbs 31:10–31. Whom do you know who reflects the virtuous purity of the Radiant Bride? How does this person's life reflect the Lord's pure, wise ways?*

- *List all of the ways the virtuous woman reflects the pure, holy heart of God himself. What is it that roots her in purity and virtue, and why is it the key that unlocks who she is as the Radiant Bride?*

🅝 WORD WEALTH

The Hebrew word used to describe this virtuous wife is *khayil*. There is no single English equivalent word, and it can be translated "mighty; wealthy; excellent; morally righteous; full of substance, integrity, abilities, and strength; mighty like an army."[76] "Woman of Valor" or "Noble Woman" is often used to describe the main character in this poem, indicating the military overtones of the word "commonly used to describe warriors, champions, and mighty ones."[77] That Proverbs concludes with a poem describing the virtuous, noble woman helps explain why the book is followed by Ruth, who herself was a virtuous, noble woman—a true *khayil*!

- *Why is this Hebrew word and all of its range of meaning the perfect word to describe the pure, virtuous woman of Proverbs 31? What does it reveal about this woman who follows after God's own heart?*

The Path of Purity

Proverbs ends with an apt appraisal of the Radiant Bride, the woman who symbolizes the purity God's children are to pursue and the virtues extolled in the entire book: "go ahead and give her the credit that is due, for she has become a radiant woman, and all her loving works of righteousness deserve to be admired at the gateways of every city!" (31:31) Read Proverbs 31:10–31 again. Then, whether you are a man or woman, pray for the wisdom to follow in this example of purity and the courage to embrace its virtue for yourself.

Talking It Out

1. What are the main areas of pleasure that trip you up, whether food, addictive substances, sexual vices, material gain, or otherwise? What role should awe-filled worship and fear of the Lord play in helping reorient those areas around the purity of the Lord and his way?

2. Have you personally struggled with alcohol or known others who drink excessively? What has that experience been like, and how might Proverbs offer wisdom for navigating alcoholic pleasures?

3. What specific false pleasures does your heart need to be emptied of? How do you long to be satisfied by Christ alone?

4. Reread Proverbs 31:10–31. What specifically do you draw from the inspiring example of the Radiant Bride, the virtuous woman? How can her example shape your own pursuit of purity in all its forms?

5. The writer of Proverbs reveals "this virtuous woman lives in the wonder, awe, and fear of the Lord," bringing this exploration on wisdom from above back to its foundation: a posture of awe-filled worship of Yahweh. What are all the things about the Lord about which you stand in awe and that lead you to worship him with holy fear? How should this shape your own life, leading you to walk in wise ways?

Endnotes

1. Brian Simmons et al., "A Note to Readers," *The Passion Translation: The New Testament with Psalms, Proverbs, and Song of Songs* (Savage, MN: BroadStreet Publishing Group, 2020), ix.

2. John Wesley, *John Wesley: Wesley's Notes on the Bible*, Christian Classics Ethereal Library, accessed January 27, 2021, https://ccel.org/ccel/wesley/notes/notes.ii.xxi.i.html.

3. Proverbs 1:1, note 'a,' TPT.

4. Didymus the Blind, Fragment 1.1, as quoted in *Proverbs, Ecclesiastes, Song of Solomon*, ed. J. Robert Wright, Ancient Christian Commentary on Scripture series, Old Testament, vol. IX (Downers Grove, IL: InterVarsity Press, 2005), 2.

5. David Maraniss, *When Pride Still Matters* (New York: Simon & Shuster, 2000), 274.

6. Proverbs 1:7, note 'a,' TPT.

7. John H. Walton and Andrew E. Hill, *Old Testament Today* (Grand Rapids, MI: Zondervan, 2013), 378.

8. John Chrysostom, Fragment 1.7, as quoted in *Proverbs, Ecclesiastes, Song of Solomon*, 7.

9. Ambrose, "Six Days of Creation," 1.4.12, as quoted in *Proverbs, Ecclesiastes, Song of Solomon*, 7.

10. Theodore of Cyrus, "Commentary on the Psalms, 14.3, as quoted in *Proverbs, Ecclesiastes, Song of Solomon*, 7.

11. Louisa M. R. Stead, "'Tis So Sweet to Trust in Jesus," 1882, public domain.

12. Proverbs 1:29, note 'c,' TPT.

13. Augustine, Sermon 348.1, Works of Augustine, as quoted in *Proverbs, Ecclesiastes, Song of Solomon*, 100.

14. Allen P. Ross, "Proverbs," in *The Expositor's Bible Commentary: Proverbs–Isaiah*, vol. 6, ed. Tremper Longman III and David E. Garland (Grand Rapids, MI: Zondervan, 2008), 135.

15. Russell K. Carter, *Standing on the Promises of God*, 1886, public domain.

16. Bruce K. Waltke, *The Book of Proverbs: Chapters 15–31* (Grand Rapids, MI: William B. Eerdmans, 2005), 202.

17. "What Is Stoicism? A Definition and 9 Stoic Exercises to Get You Started," Daily Stoic (website), accessed February 9, 2021, https://dailystoic.com/what-is-stoicism-a-definition-3-stoic-exercises-to-get-you-started.

18. Ryan Holiday and Stephen Hanselman, *The Daily Stoic: 366 Meditations on Wisdom, Perseverance, and the Art of Living* (New York: Portfolio, 2016), 4.

19. See Tremper Longman III, *Proverbs*, Baker Commentary on the Old Testament Wisdom and Psalms, ed. Tremper Longman III (Grand Rapids, MI: Baker Academic, 2006), 58–59.

20. Warren W. Wiersbe, *The Essential Everyday Bible Commentary* (Nashville, TN: Thomas Nelson, 1993).

21. Matthew Henry, Proverbs 1:20–33, *Matthew Henry's Concise Commentary,* public domain, https://biblehub.com/commentaries/proverbs/1-31.htm.

22. Paul Koptak, *The NIV Application Commentary: Proverbs* (Grand Rapids, MI: Zondervan, 2003), loc. 2724 of 20365, Kindle.

23. Ross, "Proverbs," 70–71.

24. Ross, "Proverbs," 73.

25. See Proverbs 9:17, note 'e,' TPT.

26. Ambrose, Fathers of the Church: A New Translation, as quoted in *Proverbs, Ecclesiastes, Song of Solomon*, 42.

27. Proverbs 4:23, note 'c,' TPT.

28. Proverbs 6:12–13, note 'b,' TPT.

29. Proverbs 6:16, note 'e,' TPT.

30. Bede, Corpus Christianorum, 119B:55, as quoted in *Proverbs, Ecclesiastes, Song of Solomon*, 53.

31. Chrysostom, Patrologia cursus completus, 64:685, as quoted in *Proverbs, Ecclesiastes, Song of Solomon*, 83.

32. Longman, *Proverbs*, 251.

33. Wiersbe, *The Essential Everyday Bible Commentary*, 825.

34. As translated by George Fyler Townsend, 1867, public domain, http://mythfolklore.net/aesopica/townsend/74.htm.

35. F. Brown, S. Driver, and C. Briggs, *The Brown-Driver-Briggs Hebrew and English Lexicon* (Peabody, MA: Hendrickson, 2007), 54.

36. Koptak, *Proverbs*, loc. 3864 of 20375, Kindle.

37. Longman, *Proverbs*, 239.

38. Ross, "Proverbs," 176.

39. Charles Spurgeon, Proverbs 18:12, *Morning and Evening*, public domain, https://www.biblegateway.com/devotionals/morning-and-evening/2018/03/06.

40. Spurgeon, Proverbs 18:12, *Morning and Evening*.

41. Spurgeon, Proverbs 18:12, *Morning and Evening*.

42. Spurgeon, Proverbs 18:12, *Morning and Evening*, pronouns modernized.

43. David E. Garland, *Luke*, Zondervan Exegetical Commentary Series on the New Testament, vol. 3, gen. ed. Clinton E. Arnold (Grand Rapids, MI: Zondervan, 2011), 580.

44. Garland, *Luke*, 576.

45. George William Cooke, "I've Got the Joy, Joy, Joy, Joy Down in My Heart," 1925.

46. Craig Blomberg, *Christians in an Age of Wealth* (Grand Rapids, MI: Zondervan, 2013), 81–82.

47. Spurgeon, Proverbs 11:25, *Morning and Evening*, https://www.biblegateway.com/devotionals/morning-and-evening/2014/08/21.

48. 2 Corinthians 9:6, note 'e,' TPT.

49. Cyril of Alexandria, Commentary on Luke, Homily 103, as quoted in *Proverbs, Ecclesiastes, Song of Solomon*, 126.

50. Dallas Willard, *Renewing the Christian Mind* (New York: HarperOne, 2016), 289.

51. Matthew 25:27, note 'c,' TPT.

52. Koptak, *Proverbs*, loc. 1525 of 20375, Kindle.

53. George Mobley, "Loving-Kindness," in *Eerdmans Dictionary of the Bible*, ed. David Noel Friedman (Grand Rapids, MI: Wm. B. Eerdmans, 2000), 825.

54. Mobley, "Loving-Kindness," 826.

55. Brown, Driver, Briggs, *Hebrew and English Lexicon*, 12.

56. Deuteronomy 6:5, as quoted in TPT, Matthew 22:37.

57. As quoted in TPT, Matthew 22:39.

58. Mobley, "Loving-Kindness," in *Eerdmans Dictionary of the Bible*, 826.

59. Longman, *Proverbs*, 135.

60. Koptak, *Proverbs*, loc. 3882 of 20375, Kindle.

61. Michelle Tooley, "Justice," in *Eerdmans Dictionary of the Bible*, 757.

62. Bruce Waltke, *The Book of Proverbs: Chapters 15–31* (Grand Rapids, MI: Wm. B. Eerdmans, 2005), 55.

63. Longman, *Proverbs*, 490.

64. Blomberg, *Christians in an Age of Wealth*, 81.

65. Blomberg, *Christians in an Age of Wealth*, 81–82.

66. Longman, *Proverbs*, 390.

67. "History," *Chicken Soup for the Soul* (website), accessed on April 16, 2021, https://www.chickensoup.com/about/history.

68. C. S. Lewis, *Mere Christianity* (New York: HarperOne, 1952), 47–48.

69. Spurgeon, Proverbs 24:33–34, *Morning and Evening*, https://www.biblegateway.com/devotionals/morning-and-evening/2019/11/24.

70. Koptak, *Proverbs*, loc. 14120 of 20375, Kindle.

71. Proverbs 30:21, note 'd,' TPT.

72. Longman, *Proverbs*, 531.

73. Robert Frost, "The Road Not Taken," in *Mountain Interval* (New York: Henry Holt & Co., 1916), 9.

74. Henry, Proverbs 7:6–27, *Matthew Henry's Concise Commentary*, https://biblehub.com/commentaries/proverbs/7-12.htm.

75. Gregory of Nazianzus, "Faith Gives Fullness to Reasoning: The Five Theological Orations of Gregory Nazianzen," as quoted in *Proverbs, Ecclesiastes, Song of Solomon*, 186.

76. Proverbs 31:10, note 'c,' TPT.

77. Proverbs 12:4, note 'f,' TPT.